WILLIAM McINNES

&

SARAH WATT

Worse Things Happen at Sea

hachette
AUSTRALIA

hachette
AUSTRALIA

Published in Australia and New Zealand in 2011
by Hachette Australia
(an imprint of Hachette Australia Pty Limited)
Level 17, 207 Kent Street, Sydney NSW 2000
www.hachette.com.au

Text copyright © William McInnes and Sarah Watt 2011
Photographs and illustrations copyright © Sarah Watt 2011

National Library of Australia
Cataloguing-in-Publication data

McInnes, William, 1963–
Worse things happen at sea / William McInnes and Sarah Watt.

ISBN: 978 0 7336 2802 3 (hbk.)

Families – Australia – 21st century – Anecdotes.
Australia – Social life and customs – 21st century – Anecdotes.
Watt, Sarah.

306.850994

Jacket and text design by Christa Moffitt, Christabella Designs
Cover and endpaper photographs by Sarah Watt
Set in Bembo 11/17pt
Typeset by Kirby Jones
Printed in China by South China Printing Co. Ltd.

Hachette Australia's policy is to use papers that are natural, renewable and recyclable products and made from wood grown in sustainable forests. The logging and manufacturing processes are expected to conform to the environmental regulations of the country of origin.

Contents

Little Pictures

William

Early one summer evening a year or two ago I was walking with my son, Clem, my daughter, Stella, and our dog along our street to the supermarket. Clem had a part-time job there, stacking shelves and doing the things that teenage schoolboys do at the part-time jobs they have at the local supermarket.

As we walked Stella asked me, 'Why do you always sing Dean Martin songs in the shower?'

'They're not all Dean Martin songs,' I tell her.

'Then why do they sound the same?' says Clem, laughing.

'All good songs sound like Dean Martin songs,' I say.

Both my parents liked Dean Martin. And my wife does, too. And I suppose my children have a soft spot for him; they have never openly questioned my would-be crooning in the shower.

She's just after some clarification, perhaps, is Stella, which makes me think of how we have lived in this street all my children's life. They have walked it many times and have seen it change.

Stella says to me as we cross a street, 'Remember the Cat Lady?'

The Cat Lady. I nod and say I do. As soon as she asks her question I remember.

'Mrs Budd?' says Clem.

I nod again.

We glance at the house on the corner. It has recently sold for a sum that would have seemed impossible when we first bought in this area, the home of the Cat Lady.

The Cat Lady lived in a vanilla-coloured weatherboard house that was always immaculately neat. She lived there with her husband, a man crippled by polio. He contracted it two weeks after their wedding. When we moved in I would see him shuffle in the garden on his crutches. He would hardly speak but she would wave with a friendly hesitancy.

Later, he would sit in a red motorised invalid scooter and ride the length of his fence. The whirring of the engine sounded like a Mixmaster. Once I saw him humming along the footpath, looking a little worried to be so far from home – about two hundred metres. Occasionally, after he'd grown used to his shiny contraption, he'd sit and give a little wave of his fingers as I passed. His name was, of all things, Bill. Billy Budd. It was an irony he shared the name of the hero of Melville's story of the doomed young sailor, pure of heart and youthfully beautiful, whose life is taken by the vagaries of fate.

I asked Bill Budd if he'd ever read the book *Billy Budd*.

'Nah, nah, but they called me that sometimes. Don't like the name Billy. I'm Bill.'

He didn't like a lot of things. Didn't like the dip in the footpath or the bumps on the footpath, and he didn't like a lot of the new people who had moved in.

'You, you're all right, though.' And after a while he added, 'I suppose.'

He always seemed to be dressed in grey. He grew quieter and finally he didn't wave at all; not long after, he died. Mrs Budd grew older, as did their station wagon in the lean-to garage, a Holden EH station wagon. Vanilla custard was its body colour with a white top. 'Hydromatic' in silver-plate writing on the back. I thought it was beautiful and even when rust set in, the way the colour of the silver chrome and the vanilla body dappled with the rust's brown–red still struck me as beautiful. A little picture.

One day it was gone – the Cat Lady's nephew came and took it away. She'd kept it there for him for years. She told me she was sad to see it go, it made people think that a man lived there. Kept away people with ideas. And she would nod her head. 'You know, going places they shouldn't go.'

Walking along our street I suddenly realise how lonely she must have been. Not alone, but lonely. People like me would chat to her. I remember asking her about that car as she wrestled her shopping jeep through her front gate.

'Did you ever drive it much?' I asked her.

'Oh no, no. Bill was the driver.'

Still, she was sad to see it go.

It was years later, when I would walk with Stella to her school, that the cats arrived. A few to start with and then they were everywhere. Kittens and moggies, tabbies and tortoiseshells. Half wild. Every now and then council workers would come and clear them out but then more would appear.

'They're my little kitties,' she said, immaculate in her red cardigan, yellow apron and grey dress.

One morning I saw her in tears, sobbing, gripping the top of her fence. Her wrinkled skin wrenched white around her knuckles. I asked if she was all right.

'My little kitty.'

On the road lay the body of a kitten. A car had hit it.

'My little kitty.'

I asked her if she had a bag and I went and cleaned it from the asphalt. A grey-and-white kitten. The colours of its fur were soft and deep, it weighed hardly anything. Splotches of blood were left on the road. Inside the bag the grey and white were muddied into a blur.

I looked at the red spots on the tar then went back to the Cat Lady and asked if she'd like me to bury her kitty in her yard. The yard that teemed with hissing cats.

'Oh no, no.'

I looked at her and held the plastic shopping bag filled with her little cat.

She dabbed at her eyes and said, 'It's rubbish day tomorrow.'

Well, she *was* always neat.

I nodded and popped the bag into her bin. The plastic kitty dropped onto a tidy collection of white rubbish bags. Next to the kitty bag was a box of Quaker porridge oats. An image of a chubby white-wigged man with a black hat smiled at me from the bin. I supposed he was a Quaker. It seemed to me that he looked a little bit like Alec Guinness, not in *Star Wars* mode but a more chilling John le Carré incarnation. Smiling, to be sure, but with those cold dark eyes, like a cocked pistol, staring up at me. I closed the bin.

It seemed the Cat Lady was there forever, but not quite. She fell one morning in the shower. An ambulance came and she left her house and her cats, and never came back. But the council workers did – for the cats.

I remember all that now, as I walk with my children and dog. The engine of my mind clunking along throwing stories, little pictures if you like, before my mind's eye. Her house now has a development order on it, red boxes containing plans for renovation.

Above the house a crow croaks and is chased by two smaller birds. They dart at the big bird that looks very black and heavy against the summer sky. The smaller birds loop and then fly back over the Cat Lady's house, back to their nest, and the crow flaps slowly, calls again and rests on a street light. It's startlingly beautiful, the black on the silver. Then I think of the black eyes of Alec Guinness in the Cat Lady's bin.

Little pictures everywhere.

As we walk on I think about how the houses in the street, almost all, have been or are in the process of being renovated. It is quiet but full of the activity that so many streets like this across Australia see – builders' skips full of rubbish, people in the garden finishing off the weekend by weeding and clearing, little kids playing with a foam footy and screeching at each other, a mother on the verandah looking at them and offering the advice, 'Now be nice to each other.'

Older kids use wheelie bins out in the street as wickets in a game of cricket. A car turns into the top of the street and chugs towards the players, a cracking voice calls out the timeless warning of the suburbs, 'Car coming!' and the wickets are wheeled to the side gutter to let the car pass.

Outside one house I see a plumber's van. It's a Sunday evening. If it's a call-out that will be time-and-a-half.

I laugh. It makes me think of fathers. Many years ago when I was, I realise, as old as my son is now, a friend was told by an uncle of his that if you ever wanted to get a cheap deal from a tradesman, to shake hands and press a certain knuckle on his hand.

'If he's a Freemason, mate, he'll look after you.'

I had no idea what a Mason was, but when I saw my father, Colin, I told him.

'Oh, for Christ's sake! Why would you do that?' he sighed.

'To get looked after,' I said.

My father told me that I should never pretend to be something just to gain a bit of an advantage. 'If anyone wants to be something, then let them, but just don't try and bullshit your way in to be cut a bit of slack. You do that and you're a drongo.'

I remember he shook his head and sighed again. 'Masons.'

Cut to nearly twenty years later and my son is just a toddler and my daughter is only an idea. We are renovating our house. It is a long weekend. A hot long weekend. I am digging up some of the front yard so the builders can come and do what they do. I am digging merrily away with a pick and no hat. Sarah smiles at me through the aluminium-framed windows that will soon disappear as we renovate.

'Don't you think you might need a hat?' she says.

I plunge away like a mad prospector with my pick. The soil is pretty cloggy. The pick tends to stick. I stumble a bit and trip and swear and Sarah laughs. 'Get a hat, it's hot,' she says.

I nod and see my face in the window. I look a little testy, on this Saturday when I hit a water main. Water floods. Well, these things happen. I call a plumber, he fixes it. Perhaps it is the heat. That night I lie on our bed and say to Sarah, 'I'm in a bit of strife, got a bit of sun.'

She looks at me with an expression I adore. I can hardly do it justice; it's a mixture of scornful love and mild entertainment.

'Why are you talking like somebody from a black-and-white movie?'

'Am I?'

'In a bit of strife, love.' She smiles. 'Why didn't you get a hat?'

Her eyes are wide and knowing and lovely. I smile.

'You'll be right, digger,' she says and kisses my forehead. She smells nice. Then she leaves the room to get some water and ice for me.

On the Sunday I'm back to do more damage to the claggy clay and this time I am wearing a baseball cap and swinging mightily with my pick, like Robert Redford in the film *The Natural*. I like that film, especially at the end, when Robert breaks his bat and asks the fat little batboy to pick him another. I say to myself, 'Go pick me out a winner, Bobby,' and then I swing the swing of swings. Instead of sending the ball exploding into the floodlights to win the game I hit with unerring accuracy the water main again.

These things … happen. The plumber arrives, he laughs. Time-and-a-half. He fixes the main.

It is Monday. A public holiday. Yes, it must be the heat. I'm not wearing the baseball cap now, but a white fedora-style sun hat with a rainbow-coloured hatband. These things happen in threes. My pick loves the water main. When the plumber arrives, he greets me like an old friend. 'Mate, I should take you with me! Nice hat, too!'

I look at him and I think of that knuckle. Remember it was very hot, that is why I wasn't thinking straight. The knuckle shake, he could cut me a bit of slack. I forget which one it is but press on and I shake the plumber's hand. I hang on to it.

He looks at me and I press his knuckle with my thumb. Well, perhaps if I had only pressed one, even a wrong one, it would have been all right. I, however, pressed every knuckle I could find – after all, it was double-time.

The plumber wasn't a Freemason. He looked at me and I looked at him. I held his hand and pressed a knuckle again. And smiled.

It all made sense to him. Three call-outs. Nobody could possibly be that inadequate with a pick. And who wears a white fedora with a tilted brim and rainbow hatband?

He drew his hand back as if it had been burnt and said in a rather unreconstructed tone, 'Friggin' pervert.'

He got in his truck and drove off while water seeped around me. I was indeed a drongo. I laughed and wondered why on earth I hadn't listened to my father. Perhaps that is something everyone must ask themselves at some stage. Stella asks why I was laughing and I say I was thinking of my dad and plumbers.

Fathers. We walk past the house of a man who owns little fluffy dogs. He walks them in the street. He was so proud one morning. Instead of the usual neighbourly nod he stopped me and told me how his son had, the night before, graduated as a doctor.

'We came here with almost nothing,' he said, 'and we own our home and my son, my son is a doctor. My son!' And he laughed and whistled on with his fluffy dogs.

I think of him and my own son, beside me, says, 'They had to let some people go at the supermarket last week.'

I look at him. 'Sacked them?'

He nods.

'I don't think I'd like to be sacked,' he says.

I nod.

I got the sack at the supermarket I worked at when I was a teenager. I didn't really like working there but when they let a lot of us go – funny how some things never change – I felt pretty lousy, more so than I would have thought.

That night as I lay in bed my father leant on the door to my bedroom and said in his big voice that he was proud of me and 'You'll be all right,' and he ambled off, half-humming, half-singing a Dean Martin tune, 'Send Me the Pillow that You Dream On'.

I thought of that and so I punch Clem in the arm and say, 'You'll be all right.'

Clem just laughs and shakes his head.

We stop outside a house. It, too, is being renovated. All the cladding has gone and the handmade garden statues have been parked out the front in the middle of bits of plaster and wall, Snow White with her eyes too close together and a collection of weird-looking dwarves. They stand forlornly, victims of planned disaster. And there, too, is a shower. Not just the head but the whole shower casing, dull ruby pink with soap holder and taps and invalid handles. The old man who had lived here would slowly pedal his bicycle around the streets with a woman walking beside him. She was his daughter.

'Not bad for eighty-nine, eh?' he would say to me and his daughter would laugh.

I saw them once outside the house. He was having trouble getting on the bike and she stood beside him, gently holding his elbow. He seemed a bit cranky, in fact he was always a touch cranky.

'All right, all right,' he snapped.

'Go easy, Dad,' his daughter said softly.

I asked if they needed a hand. The old man didn't say anything. His daughter said they were fine. The old man then held his daughter's hand. He squeezed it.

'You remember when we made those things?' he said. He nodded his head towards Snow White.

'Yes, Dad.' His daughter laughed. 'You shouted so much. And I still think her eyes are too close together.'

Her father smiled a little and she helped him on the bike.

'Not bad for eighty-nine, eh?' she said to me about her father. She said it with pride.

'No, not bad at all,' I said.

Fathers and children.

'Poor old Snow White,' says Stella. 'They're throwing her out,' and I hold her hand.

Yes, the street is changing. The old man had died a year or two before. New people were living in his house. Well, they were in their new home. And they were renovating it. We are all too often led down the convenient path that makes us think we can somehow manage time, that we have time to put things off and deal with stuff later. We fill our days with things that seemingly stretch on forever – mortgages that must be paid, jobs that must be attended to, traditions to which we must adhere.

But life isn't like that. It goes on and we go with it, to a point. We are finite.

I walk along our street with my children. Clem is already taller than me and Stella is growing up. I am growing older. Life goes on, just look at the street.

I think of the first time Sarah and I walked into the house that would become our home. It was dark and musty. A grey paisley carpet ran through the living room and bedrooms. On top of a wardrobe in the main bedroom was a packet of Claridge cigarettes. Maroon and gold. It lay unopened. The kitchen had a lino floor, grey with flashes of colour whipped through – yellow and red, plus little diamonds of blue.

As I walk I think about that lino and that it was quite beautiful.

The house was a rabbit warren of cupboards and shelving and at the back a low skillion roof contained a toilet and fernery. The toilet was obviously an outhouse that had been built in. On top of its slanted roof I found an old *Truth* newspaper, covered in

to of an American dancer, who at that time was
ith a forty-eight-inch bust and inside the paper
r time enjoying Australia. Whoever had put it
he back was a piece about how Captain Blood
ys were up to the task of making the finals. The
he exotic dancer's cover.
of the toilet roof. Who had put it there remained
one's life and worth enough to hide in the secret
fifteen years. A bit of private reading matter for

the bricks with the Olympic rings on the sides.
Sarah and her friend put in a huge support beam
up the back. Chocked up with a car-tyre jack,
eam loomed above. I had no role in this part of
Sarah and her friend. I stood back and looked at
was seven months pregnant. As they posed for a
le, 'Do you think it's safe?'
ieir home in the house in which we live.

---

alked along the dark hall of our home. Clem was
on the couch in the living room and made a
way the pages of the book he was supposed to be

with my basket of dry washing. 'Just read it,' and
ik commercial from the seventies: 'Go on, Freddy

---

3. How to take Atorvastatin Tablets
4. Possible side effects
5. How to store Atorvastatin Tablets
6. Further information

1. WHAT ATORVASTATIN TABLETS ARE AND WHAT THEY ARE USED FOR

Atorvastatin belongs to a group of medicines known as statins, which are lipid (fat) regulating medicines.

Atorvastatin is used to lower lipids known as cholesterol and triglycerides in the blood when a low fat diet and life style changes on their own have failed. If you are at an increased risk of heart disease, Atorvastatin can also be used to reduce such risk even if your cholesterol levels are normal. You should maintain a standard cholesterol lowering diet during treatment.

2. BEFORE YOU TAKE ATORVASTATIN TABLETS

Do not take Atorvastatin Tablets
• if you are hypersensitive (allergic) to atorvastatin or to any

Please tell your doctor or pharmacist if you are taking or have recently taken any other medicines, including medicines obtained without a prescription.

Taking Atorvastatin Tablets with food and drink
See Section 3 for instructions on how to take Atorvastatin Tablets. Please note the following:

Grapefruit juice
Do not take more than one or two small glasses of grapefruit juice per day because large quantities of grapefruit juice can change the effects of atorvastatin.

Alcohol
Avoid drinking too much alcohol while taking this medicine. See Section 2 "Take special care with Atorvastatin Tablets" for details

Pregnancy and breast-feeding
Do not take Atorvastatin Tablets if you are pregnant, or if you are trying to become pregnant.
Do not take Atorvastatin Tablets if you are able to become

drink it … Drink it! Drink it!' I remembered that almost as soon as I said it. 'A glass of milk is like a big white vitamin pill, so go on, Freddy, drink. Drink it!'

Then an unseen hand, a mother's hand, would put a tablespoon of Quik in the glass of milk. It was sweet stuff. Chocolate or strawberry flavour. I liked strawberry better – I used to put heaped spoonfuls into glasses with an embossed Cobb & Co. coach on them, they used to be jam jars. My mother would go spare at me because I would use so much. It had shiny bits in it, like specks of glass, and I would see them sparkle almost hypnotically as I heaped away. I'd use so much of this powder that it wouldn't last a week. Five kids and one tin of Quik per week. My mother would hold up the tin and tell me I was using too much, that everyone had to have some, it wasn't fair.

That didn't really stick with me, I liked the shiny bits of powder.

Then she tried fear tactics. 'It's sugar, all sugar. It'll rot your teeth.'

I'd stare at her.

'You'll have no teeth left, none at all!'

I'd stare.

'You'll have to go to the *dentist*!'

I hated the dentist. And away they went, the little pictures in my mind as I walked along our hallway. Barbers and dentists. They smelt funny and smiled, pretending to be friendly, but both soon got very cranky, so it was little wonder I'd always get dentists and barbers mixed up. Both wore white coats, both made you sit in weird chairs that lifted off the ground and their places of work had peculiar smells.

There were subtle differences, though. Take reading matter: go to the barber and you'd see the *Australasian Post* with a smiling girl on a beach sucking her stomach in and fishing magazines with fish and blokes sticking their guts out; the dentist would have Little Golden Books or *The Bulletin*. And the dentist would never call you Champ or Digger.

My present dentist is as old as Moses and is just as good with commandments.

'Floss! Floss! Floss! You must respect your teeth!' He sings opera and makes more racket than Chinese New Year – an attempt to take his patient's mind off what he is doing inside their mouth.

He's also a master of the Dentalise language. No matter how numb your tongue is or how many of those little white rolls of cotton are wedged in your gob he can understand your grunts, mumbles and other noises.

Many years ago in Bondi, a Russian-born dentist, who had an outrageous accent like a baddie from a Roger Moore Bond film, made about as much sense as I did as she tried to prise a wisdom tooth from my jaw, yet she still managed to natter on in answer to my whimpers.

I groaned. She nodded in agreement.

'Needink more leveeeragge.'

With that she put a knee on my chest and pulled for all she was worth. In many ways a very intimate moment. Her face was centimetres from mine and it was twisted in effort. She bared her teeth and roared with the strain then success, howling, 'Toot! Tooooooot!'

She held aloft something that had been embedded in my skull. 'Toooot!'

I nodded and said, 'Ooooooood.'

She looked at me. 'Nyet, toot.'

Strange thing about dentists – we only see them from the patient's view. Ever thought what it's like to stare down into someone's mouth?

Once, fielding at third slip, I noticed that Gary, who stood at second slip, grimaced, coughed and shook his hands.

'You right?' I asked.

He coughed. Again. He shook his head. 'Bit of a flashback. Glasgow. Mr James, 10.30 appointment.'

At the drinks break Gary filled me in. He'd been a dentist for the National Health Service in Britain and he still remembered a particular 10.30 appointment.

'Mate, when that old fellow opened his mouth and breathed it was like unleashing the hounds of hell and his teeth were all over the place like a mad woman's proverbial.' He shivered. 'Should've gone into business with my dad,' he said.

'What was he?'

'A barber.'

As I thought about my mother yelling at me I knew even then that I disliked the dentist more than the barber. And my mother knew this, so she let rip with the big guns. Or gums.

'Teeth,' she said, pointing to her own. 'The dentist will pull them out. One by one.' She pointed to my teeth. 'One by one!' and she slowly took her bottom plate out. 'One!' she yelled. And then she slipped out her top plate. 'By one!' And she bared her gums with their two remaining teeth.

I stared and then she roared. 'I want six pounds of sausages!' she said and she didn't sound like her. Two teeth and pink gums. 'I want thith poundth of beef thausageth!'

There was a silence and then she burst out laughing.

That's what I thought as I walked down the hallway, all over in only a few steps. How quickly the mind pieces images and memory together.

I yelled to Clem, 'Go on, Freddy, drink it!'

He had no idea what I meant, but that's not the point.

The front door opened and into our home walked a man I had never seen before.

I stopped in the hallway, wearing my PJs with planets of the universe plastered over them (a Father's Day present) and carrying my white plastic washing basket. And I stared.

He came in with a sense of familiarity that surprised me. He looked at me, nodded and half turned to carefully close the door.

'Oh,' he said with some relief. 'That's better.'

'You right?' was what I came up with in reply.

He had long hair and a drooping moustache. He stared back at me.

'Yeah, I am now,' he said in a sort of wounded tone.

My son said from the couch, 'Who's Freddy?'

The man with the moustache said, 'It's not me,' and took a few steps down the hall.

'Mate,' I said.

'Are you Freddy?' he said.

'No, no, I'm not. I think you may have the wrong house.'

He stared at me. 'Fred, that's my room down there on the left, down the hall.'

I shook my head and puffed out my chest and washing basket.

He looked at me and my laundry. 'Isn't this the boarding house?'

'No,' I said. 'This is not the boarding house.'

His shoulders sank a bit and then he was quite apologetic. 'Mate, I'm so sorry, Freddy. Mate, I don't know where I am. I've been walking around for hours; I'm a bit lost. Silly as a wheel, it's the medicine. Got a brain tumour. I'm just a bit bloody stupid.'

I put down my washing basket and told him that it was fine. I'd give him a lift to the boarding house, which wasn't that far.

We got in the car and he said sorry again. I told him it was fine.

'Had my own house once,' he said, 'but that was a different life.'

I nodded and thought I should say something. 'I suppose we all have different lives.'

He looked at me. 'You, you are still in your pyjamas and it's past midday, Freddy. You want to get your act together a bit. Don't want to waste the day.'

He tapped the roof of the car before he left and I looked after him.

I could have thought many things but all that came to me was, That bloke thinks my home looks like a boarding house.

I have seen that fellow since, walking the streets, sometimes going into the right boarding house, sometimes just walking, and I have thought of that idea of different lives. Do we all have them? Or is it more a case of how quickly a mind can stream through memory and events? Pictures from our past, some imagined and some borrowed, can float through our lives as we live them.

It's not amazing to remember a television commercial from over forty years ago, but to appropriate it and make it a part of an incident in the hallway of my home strikes me as being amazing in an un-amazing way. That man still says, 'Hello, Fred,' to me occasionally.

Yet memories and images are seldom random. They can fly from the past and dance with the present but there is a connection in them that's a wonder.

Even though a street and a house may change, and life charges on, there are some things that always stay the same. The bond between a father and his children. I think of the man and his fluffy dogs and how proud he was of his son, how his son had given so much to his father. I think of the father and daughter and how all those years after they had made the garden statues he reached for her hand and held it and how she steadied him and how proud she was of him.

Nobody has the secret to being a parent, just as nobody has the secret to living, no matter how many self-help and life-guidance books are published. Nobody is the perfect parent. All we can do is be with the people we care about and think of them.

My father, like me I suppose, would yell and carry on. I am more impatient than he was, even though he had five children. And when I think about it, maybe he never really yelled at us that much. I yell a little too easily, perhaps.

'You think I yell too much?' I ask Clem.

He looks at me. He's wearing a blue shirt for work and it makes his eyes seem even bluer. 'Are you serious?'

It's his eyes. I see them and I feel a hot plastic chair. North Queensland with the remnants of a warm shandy in my glass gives me a chance to ponder my position. First I ask myself what in God's name made me think that the island I chose for our winter holiday would really be the blue-skied wonderland of the brochures. *Paradise for parents, heaven for kids.* That is what the brochures had said about this spot of rock in the warm seas of Queensland.

Next time you happen to be in a shopping centre at Christmas-time, do me this favour: close your eyes and listen — children screaming, crying, yelling, squealing and laughing, muzak playing and amplified and meaningless noise. Hear various children's names rattled out of parents' mouths and the assorted threats that follow. That's what our winter holiday sounded like.

Yes, I'm sitting by the pool on a plastic chair that sticks to my legs as I try to stand. I sit next to my brother, Vaughan, who looks at me blankly, trying to divvy up who was responsible for a joint family holiday to this playground in the sun.

We are by the pool because we are on pool duty. Our children, my Clem and Vaughan's son and two daughters, are in the pool. Sometimes. Other times they run howling around its edge and plunge, giggling, into the water. The pool teems with toddlers, like a creek teems with tadpoles after the rains. And like tadpoles they appear to be identical, wet, beaming little beings of joy. That is until one of the little tadpoles steals another's floaties or air-ring or ball. Then various tired parents do their best to calm beating breasts and sobbing sons or daughters.

It is a fact of such holidays that there always happen to be some children whose sole job is to make a bad situation worse. These are the children who appear to be parentless, for when some form of discipline is required and you tell them not to push people's heads under the water and to go back to their mum or dad, they rush back into the maelstrom of the pool. No one puts their hand up for ownership of these kids; they are simply forces of nature – a bit like cyclones.

Fatherhood. This is a part of it, a part that must be lived through. Pool duty on a holiday. Not all beer and skittles. Times like this make Vaughan and me remember our father's withering glare and vengeful warning, as we would hoon around the dinner table and generally drive him around the bend.

'You two gooses just wait until you have kids – you won't know what's bloody hit you.'

Picture those two brothers now with the same thought in their hearts: Dad, we know what you mean. We are sorry, we are sorry.

And yet just when the noise seems maddening, when the antics of the forces of nature seem so fearful, when the warm shandy in your hands is raised to your lips and you notice a particularly vile fly the size of your thumb floating in the froth … When things can get no worse, a miracle occurs. A sweet little voice is heard. Above the other racket it calls to you. 'Daddy! Daddy!'

And there, arms outstretched, little blue eyes blazing with life and love and joy and filled with everything good in life, is your child. My little son. Wet from the pool and followed by his cousins he splashes towards me. He runs, as do his cousins, with the fragile fluttering movements reserved for truly beautiful things like butterflies and children.

'Daddy, Daddy,' whispers the little voice in my ear, 'I love you.'

My brother is draped with his children and he smiles over at me. We are both thinking of our father and we both know that in that one instant, blanketed in the unmasking and unsullied love of our children, we have never had such a fine holiday. That is the wonder, the real majesty of fatherhood, of knowing that the little bundle in my arms is my child. I marvel that I hold something so beautiful and have that beauty say it loves me.

It is enough to make grey skies turn as blue as his eyes and it is enough to turn this spot of rock in the waters of Queensland into a jewelled paradise.

And here he is beside me on the street now, tufts of hair on his face, taller than me, smiling. He shakes his head and laughs. At me. 'No, Dad, you don't yell too much.'

Stella shakes her head.

Maybe my father didn't yell that much. I have a little picture of him in my mind as we walk. He had a habit of bursting out with, 'Ahoy! You!' to one of us children and then giving one of us a bear hug and telling us that he was proud of us and that he loved us.

I never knew why he did it, but as I walk with my kids and our dog I think I now know. Life goes by, we grow and change, but if we care and let those we love know that we do, then maybe some things will always remain strong.

'Hey, you two,' I say and I try to sing a Dean Martin song. The dog barks and I yell.

Mothers

William

Mothers teach you lots of things – how to mind your manners, how to brush your teeth, how not to pick your nose. And sometimes they can teach you how to die.

My mum died in April of 2010. In Brisbane General Hospital after being there for nearly six months. I rang her quite a bit – perhaps not as much as I could have, but whenever she answered she would assure me she was on the up and up and only a few days away from walking out, back to Redcliffe, back to the beach and her two mad dogs, Blodwyn and George.

We all came to visit and would bring little treats and gifts. Her three daughters: Laurie would bring old Robert Donat films and Rhian, flowers. Corby would bustle in after work and share stories from her day. The trivia club ladies gave her chocolates and cuttings from newspapers. Sarah once brought some calendula cream and rubbed it onto my mother's hands.

'Oh yum,' said my mother. 'Hands that say I love you.'

I looked at them, Sarah holding the old hands of my mother – I knew the touch of both and when I saw them entwined I felt an odd mix of emotion, a surge of sadness, happiness and acceptance. But I think it was love I felt most of all.

I just brought myself, mostly, but Vaughan topped the pops when he brought in some 'Midsomer Murders' DVDs, the English television show set in some mythical county of murderous villages. The chief protagonist was a Chief Inspector Barnaby, whose arms were astoundingly short.

'Like he'd pinched them off a midget wrestler,' my mother once mumbled. She would delight in its entertaining absurdity, though. 'Watched old Short Arms himself and that cow of a wife of his!' she nattered away down the phone to me during one call.

And Eileen Kendall, an old friend of Mum's, would drop off Mary MacKillop postcards and dab her forehead with a dampened hanky dipped into a jar of water that she had brought back from Lourdes.

'She's got a bleeding beer fridge full of that stuff, you know,' said Mum. 'God bless her.'

Sometimes she'd walk around the ward slowly, dropping in and chatting to other patients, discovering new characters in the beds next to her. There was the woman who'd moan through the day and night: 'The poor thing sounds like a mix between an air-raid siren and Rudy Vallee,' my mum would explain.

Then there was the deaf farmer bellowing in his sleep about fences and slip rails and the roof on his shed.

And best of all was the woman who had been flown down from Rockhampton and who, for that reason, my mother christened Rocky. She was forever mispronouncing words, to Mum's delight, and my mother loved to collect them.

'Oh, old Rocky told me one morning she was being prepared for surgery. "They're going to put a kanaka in me mouth but it hurts because of me Hermes." The poor old cow meant the cannula [the medical draining tube] was hurting her cold sore,' roared my mother.

But as the days went by she couldn't walk as far and the treatment wasn't as successful as was hoped. One week turned into two and then into a month. She changed rooms a couple of times, but that ward became her last home.

Soon it was time for all her children, her daughters-in-law and her friends to gather around her bedside and it was here, we came to understand, that her life would end. In a small room five floors up.

I watched her once as she slept, and my mind flew to the moment some years before, when I found myself hanging upside down, then falling from a high precipice, my hands burning as hot nylon rope slipped through my fingers. Green slimy liquid oozed around my feet as I skidded and desperately skated across a hard surface, frantically trying to gain some foothold. I tilted crazily and before my eyes flashed the sun, the blue sky and then my life. Then I heard a booming voice. My mother's voice.

'William, when did Matt Munro … William … Oh, you stupid boy.'

I was painting my mother's roof. Why, I don't know. I was supposed to be on holiday. Somehow Sarah had got it into her head that we could have a holiday in Redcliffe at my mother's house and help fix and tidy things up a bit.

We arrived and placed Clem into the school that my siblings and I had all attended, Humpybong Infants, for a couple of weeks and went to work – or 'the fix-up'.

Sarah loves a job, a task, and she dragged me and my mother along. Well, not exactly my mum. She was a bit perplexed, happy stuff was being done, but I think she was a little surprised that one of her daughters-in-law thought that it would be a fun way to spend time.

As for me, I tried to do as little as possible, seeping comfortably into the role of the youngest of the family.

But my mother soon got into the swing of things. She said she liked the noise, the hammering. It reminded her of my dad. She'd be sitting doing a jigsaw with Stella at the big table and she'd look up and get misty-eyed as the house rang with a hammer belting a nail into the lengths of timber from which my dad had fashioned the home.

'Oh, doesn't that sound lovely?'

Sarah went off and busied herself with building sets of shelves and painting the upstairs area and discovered that she had a kindred spirit in the carpentry work of my father.

My old man had extended and renovated the big house in which I'd grown up, following his own peculiar style of design. He'd find a piece of wood he liked and then build the house around it. In many ways it was like a jigsaw puzzle, and once you recognised the method you could appreciate what he had been up to.

Sometimes Sarah would laugh or emit a long 'Oh' of understanding at what had somehow been stuck and matched together. She'd planned the first renovation of our home in the same manner, by the rule of thumb and eye. It's startling to look at our home now and see how similar it is in spirit to the one where I grew up. That rule of 'design by eye' produced something my father would have appreciated: a tough Astro Turf putting lawn of about thirty-five square metres. Fed up with weeds growing through the concrete slab that I had poured with my mate Leon – a slab that started off promisingly but had deteriorated into a three-dimensional relief map of the Andes with each beer we sipped and the closer it came to the start of the footy match between Footscray and Carlton – Sarah decided to buy synthetic lawn. This naturally led to the idea of creating our own mini-golf course.

The morning of the day of one of Sarah's last rounds of chemo treatment a bearded man, looking not unlike James Last – the bearded, wind-blown, easy-listening orchestra conductor of the seventies – knocked on our door, straining like a weightlifter. He panted and the veins in his neck bulged. He heaved a few deep breaths and then very politely apologised for arriving so early with the delivery of our turf, but it was a busy day for him.

I assured him that it was all right; my son would give him a hand.

He heaved a bit more and said in the same polite manner that 'It might be an idea if you grabbed a few neighbours.' Sweat beaded from him.

I told him I'd give him a hand as well.

I got Clem out of bed, which is no easy thing to accomplish quickly.

Sometimes it takes a lot to get out of bed. A couple of things can help. One uni holiday break I generously returned home to my parents to eat as much as I could and sleep for a month. Dad called me Double Digit Bill – I never left the cocoon of bed before the clock reached double figures. Mum would exercise her vocal abilities, trying to raise me to the land of the living.

'You're sleeping your day away, you buffoon!' she'd boom until she worked out a more effective method – a water pistol filled from the water jug in the fridge. She squirted me a blast. It must have looked like a deleted scene from *Dirty Harry*; Dirty Harry dressed as my mother, standing over me with a long-barrelled magnum, growling, 'Are you getting up, punk, or you want some more?'

'Go on, let him have it!' my father encouraged from behind his newspaper.

After a few mornings, the mere hint of a Dirty Harry wake-up was enough.

Once, when a friend came round and I was still in bed, Dirty Mummy uttered a memorable line. 'Let me get my gun and I'll wake him up for you.'

I was out of the house in less than ten minutes.

When I wake my children I use threats. Never had to use the Dirty Harry wake-up yet. Saying I'm going to sing does the trick. The threat of Dean Martin crossed with old Brisbane rugby league team songs is mighty powerful. How could a blend of 'Somewhere There's a Someone' and the tune of 'Past Brothers' (a bowdlerised Irish jig), go wrong?

> *'Well now, Brothers, the team on which we depend, are valiant*
> > *and gallant right to the end.*
> *Against them the other teams just do not rate,*
> *They're the strongest in Brisbane — the cream of the state.*
> *It's the blue and the white, it's the team of the brothers,*
> *The team that's superior to all the others,' et cetera.*

But not this morning, no footy tunes or Dean-o. I walked into my son's room and shook him. 'Clem. Clem! *Clem!*' He cavemanned a grunt at me.

'Clem, the man with the grass is here.'

'That's like a line out of a really bad movie, Dad,' he said.

'Get up. Come on, it's the fake grass.'

'Oh, you owe me,' he muttered and we reported for duty in our pyjamas.

What met us was a roll of whatever it is that fake turf is made from, measuring the width and size of a giant tree trunk.

'Whoa!' said Clem.

'Hmm,' said the polite turf-lifter.

'Shit,' I said.

'Hmm,' said the polite turf-lifter again.

Somehow with great effort we managed to carry the turf trunk in fits and bursts off the ute, up the stairs, down the hall and out the back.

The ute was the worst. I'd barely cleared the sleep from my eyes, and the weight was forbidding. Grunting and growling and shrieking, Clem and I slipped in our Croc-clad feet, while the impassive turf-lifter said quietly, 'Are you right?' repeatedly.

An old man walking a greyhound stopped, looked and laughed. 'You blokes sound like Elvis the last time he went to crap in the dunny. You got a whole lot of shaking going on.'

'Thank you very much,' said Clem in a brave attempt at an Elvis.

Through the hall, I whispered, 'Quiet! Don't wake Mum,' and then proceeded to howl as I clipped my head on the hallstand and shout when one of the plastic Viking hats hanging on to it toppled into my nose.

The dog, of course, barked like a maniac.

For the tenth time the turf-lifter asked, 'Are you right?'

He was immensely strong and impassive in an almost otherworldly manner. Perhaps he was heavily medicated. Perhaps not. But he intoned the words like a meditative chant.

While Clem and I stopped and dropped the turf trunk, his neck bulged. He took a breath and held up his end of the bargain. His eyes were like ping-pong balls by the time we reached the end of the hall. They were the size of tennis balls by the time we got through the glass doors and past the washing and over the dog's bowl. The only time his calmness looked like breaking was when he backed into Clem's cricket ball on a long string that was tied to the pagoda. Clem and I use this to smack the ball with a cricket bat from time to time. It makes a pleasing sort of sound against the willow and you can tell when you've hit that mythic sweet spot. The ball had been thumped and had curled around the pagoda's beam at an unfortunate head-hunting height.

When the turf-lifter bunted it with the back of his head he released a strangled, 'Ah!'

'It's hit the sweet spot,' I said and Clem rose to the occasion by asking him very calmly, 'Are you right?'

I dropped the turf trunk on my feet. The turf-lifter looked at me.

'Where are you going to lay the lawn?' he said, quietly.

'Here,' and I pointed to the slab of the Andes.

The turf-lifter smiled. His eyes had returned to their rightful size. He had sharp little teeth.

'You'll never do it, matey. Good luck to you,' he said and walked into the ball again.

We contained ourselves this time and offered him a tea or coffee but he had to be off and deliver more turf.

'Tough job,' I said.

The cricket ball swung perilously close to his head but missed. Turf-lifter looked at us and then grabbed the cricket ball, steadied it from swinging and then let it hang loose in the morning sun. He turned to us.

'Well, it's what I do,' he said and with a nod in our direction he added, 'You meet all types. Nice to get out.' And then he and his impassive strength walked out the door and into his day.

This is when Sarah emerged in her pyjamas, cowboys and Indians printed on them, and proceeded to direct the laying of the turf.

She used the famous rule of thumb and eye to install the lawn within an hour. Measuring the space with a foam garden knee pad – 'Tape measures are for wimps' – we fitted the lawn and stood back to marvel at our work.

Clem took in the tough-turf view and then held the knee pad in his hands and admired it and his mother.

'You know, Mum, someone like you would have built the pyramids.'

'Out of Astro Turf,' I said.

I made five holes in the grass and concrete beneath, popped in paper cups and went off to the op shop to find suitable mini-golf obstacles. The best were two plaster Egyptian statues.

The girl at the checkout looked at them and said approvingly, 'These are very powerful spiritually, you know.'

She held them up and on the bottom I saw 'Savers $9.99'.

I nodded and went back to our mini-golf backyard, stuck them on an upturned box and christened that particular part of the course the Hole of the Pharaohs.

Clem was impressed. 'You see, Mum, you *could* have built the pyramids.' Then he said, 'Putt-putt? Mini-golf!' and laughed.

When Clem was smaller and visiting my mother, she would take him to the mini-golf course on the banks of Humpybong Creek, across from the old Catholic church. It was your classic mini-golf course with plaster-and-wood windmills and cows and helicopters and kangaroos strewn about the holes. My mother liked it except for the name.

'Too American. It's not bloody putt-putt, it's mini-golf. We're here for a game of mini-golf,' she would say to the rather uninterested woman behind the till. 'We're not buying any hotdogs from her,' muttered my mother as she grabbed a putter and headed for the first hole.

Clem liked it as much for the nonsense his nanna carried on with as for hitting a ball with a stick. Once, Mum had squatted down by the fibreglasses cow and pretended to milk it.

'No milk today? Come on, you lazy moo. No, she's as dry as. We'll have to buy some sars.'

Her little grandson would stare and then get the joke and clap his hands. Whenever his Nanna Mac milked the fibreglass moo, he knew he'd end up with a glass of sarsaparilla.

Staring at the Hole of the Pharaohs now, Clem laughed his big barking howl, like my father used to do. 'It's not putt-putt! Too American. It's mini-golf!'

'I wonder what happened to those cows?' he asked me. Then he went inside to raid the fridge.

It was no surprise to me then that Sarah would appreciatively belt away with hammer and nail, but the idea of me painting the roof was not something I was keen to actually make happen.

I told Mum I'd pay to have the roof done.

'Oh,' she said, 'it's not the same.'

The same as what? Having a job professionally done as opposed to seeing your youngest child nearly strangle himself and choke on green roof paint?

'Sarah is painting and banging away. She didn't have to be asked.'

I see. My mother had asked. Me. That was different. Maybe she wanted a bit of entertainment in between jigsaws and watching Tyrone Power movies with Stella.

The roof used to be my dad's sole province – he'd disappear up there, sit on its crest and look around the neighbourhood and out across the bay. My mother didn't like heights and so whenever she wanted to talk to him she would yell and he would yell back. What they'd both yell wasn't what one would normally expect to be yelled. Here, I'm supposing that something yelled would maybe be along the lines of an oath, a scream of shock, a cavalry officer roaring 'Charge!' Yes, maybe a touch of Mel Gibson in the more frantic moments of *Braveheart*. But that was the manner in which my parents would communicate while engaging in chitchat.

'Cup of tea, love?' Mum would *Braveheart*.

'Wha –? You what?' Dad would Cavalry Officer.

'A cup of tea!'

'Ta very much, love. Lovely out on the bay!' he'd *Braveheart* back.

Perhaps that's why my mother wanted me up on the roof; she wanted to have a roared conversation, a bit of *Braveheart* chitchat. Or maybe she wanted to see if I'd sound like him. Maybe that's why she was *Braveheart*ing about Matt Monro.

'When did Matt Monro play at the Redcliffe Entertainment Centre?'

Her roaring at me while I scrambled up on the roof unsettled me. I had a chance to *Braveheart* back, but I slipped and the rope bit into my arse and I screamed. Actually, I yelped. And hanging there, looking at her from my crazy viewpoint atop the house in Redcliffe where I grew up, as I decided whether to scream or pray, I thought, everyone has one. You can't say you don't and really, why would you want to? I looked at mine: Mum. I've known her all my life and there is something to be said for that as it flashes past your eyes.

As a little boy, I remember tripping as I played in the backyard and crying. And arms picking me up and brushing away tears. Her making banana-and-sugar sandwiches and cups of weak tea for me as a treat.

'Don't fuss, here's your smoko lunch,' she would say and I'd sit at the back door and chat to the cat. Every now and then her hand would stroke my head. Maybe in the background Matt Monro or Dean Martin or one of her favourite crooners would warble from the stereo. There was always music.

I thought of her, this woman, this mother of mine, singing the chooky-chook song as we fed her chooks deep in the darkest part of our backyard. I remember how she would take me shopping, plonking me in the trolley and pushing me around the aisles and talking to me occasionally, in between conversations she'd have with other women.

'This is the youngest, then?' a voice would say.

I'd look up and see various faces, some with purple hair, some old, some a little like my mother.

'Yes, this is the youngest,' my mother would say as a hand floated down and stroked my head.

Yes, the youngest of five and apparently the longest to deliver if my mother's claims are anything to go by. I remember, in my adolescence, happily squeezing blackheads and letting rip on the back verandah and turning to see if the dog appreciated my efforts. I saw my mother.

'Nineteen bloody hours it took to have you, and look at you.'

Whenever I did anything wrong or stupid, which was quite frankly often, my father would yell to Mum, 'Look what your silly bloody son's gone and done!'

And my mum would look me square in the eye and mutter, 'Nineteen hours.'

Whenever I did do something stupid, though, they were always there and my mum would somehow sort it out. In fact, now that I think of it, I realise I never doubted that she would be there.

I called out to her once when I was walking home from Humpybong little school. I felt very grown-up. I called but she didn't hear. I called again – was she there? I felt a rising panic. And I felt not so grown-up. And I shrieked for to her to come and help me cross Oxley Avenue and … she came. She waved to me from the high window of our house and came over to guide me through the traffic. She was always there.

I thought about how she cared for my father, a man she had known and loved; a man who was taken from her by the ravages of cancer and Alzheimer's. She was with him as long as he had it. She never left his side. She took him on last visits to the places of his childhood, to his brother in Canada, and held him as she walked with him around the old battlefields in Europe where he had fought in the Second World War.

On one street corner in Holland she couldn't get him to walk across the street. She tried to cajole him, then to push and finally she gave up and so he stood there, clinging to the side of a building, a man lost in the haze of dementia. Later, when they were visiting a friend of my father's in Ireland my mother told the man of this incident. He had fought with Dad during the War and he looked at my mother and then slowly got up and went to my father and cuddled him. That is what my mother said he did. 'Got up and cuddled your father. And then he said, "You remembered that corner, Col, didn't you?"'

My father's old friend told my mother that an enemy sniper had picked off members of a paratrooper squad and my father had held men back and pulled them into the wall of the building on the corner to protect them, including the old friend who cuddled him all those years later.

'Funny, the old bugger remembering that,' my mother said.

She never travelled well, even though she did embark on some big trips. She was, however, inventive when it came to safety and travel.

During her time as president of the craft club at the Redcliffe Pensioners Association she had cause, for some reason, to make a life-sized doll dressed in a sailor's suit, complete with bell-bottom trousers and striped jumper, purchased from an army disposals store. This sailor, who had a big moon face made from a stuffed nylon stocking and drawn-on paper eyes and a bushy beard courtesy of a dyed red mop, accompanied Mum on a trip to Sydney to visit Laurie, my sister. She struck upon the idea that if she stuffed Jolly

Jack Tar in the passenger's seat of her canary-yellow Volvo she'd be safer, people seeing an elderly woman and a big strapping fellow driving together. The fact that Jolly Jack Tar was the size and shape of Haystacks Calhoun made the car look, in my mother's words, as though it belonged to one of those awful 'simple' families that you'd see on 'Today Tonight'.

Jolly Jack, because of his lack of a skeleton, had the unfortunate habit of keeling over and toppling into my mother's lap while she was driving. She'd swerve, swear and hoick Jolly Jack by his red locks and in annoyance shake his head and sometimes slap him back into position. Some motorists and onlookers didn't quite get a clear picture of what she was up to.

I received a very odd look from one man who wanted to clean my windscreen at an intersection in Sydney after I'd given Jolly Jack what for. The fellow just stared at me with his gob open.

But my sailor-monstering mum reached her destination safely enough and returned home – this time with Jolly Jack strapped in the back seat.

I think of the laughter she's given me. Of the card I received when she went trekking through Nepal and the Himalayas and hoping that when I was her age – she was well over seventy – I'd be courageous enough to do the same. I thought of her coming with me to the Melbourne Cup. At the end of the day, after much champagne and no winners, how I cried with laughter as I walked home with her. My mum.

Once, when Clem and I were visiting her, when he was very young as opposed to the giant adolescent he is now, my young boy tripped and fell as he played cowboys with Mum's dogs in the backyard. He began to cry and before I reached him my mum had taken him in hand and was educating him in the ways of good cowboy movies and bad cowboy movies. Errol Flynn and Gregory Peck were the go, Burt Lancaster and Richard Widmark were good, but on no accounts should he ever watch anything with Cornel Wilde in it. She proceeded to do an impersonation of whoever Cornel Wilde was.

We both laughed and Clem looked at us and laughed, too. He didn't understand what my mother was saying but he knew his Nanna Mac was being funny, being silly

and making everything good. She stood up and let her hand float down and stroke his head.

'Would you like some banana-and-sugar sandwiches? A cowboy has to have his smoko lunch.'

I loved her very much when she did that. But I didn't tell her, didn't want to make a fuss.

So as I hung off that roof with paint going everywhere and I looked down at her, I thought of what a cracker she is. What a terrific mum. My mum. But I didn't tell her, didn't want to make a fuss.

'You,' she said with a melodramatic sneer. 'You yelping fool!'

We proceeded to have an argument over when Matt Monro sang at the Redcliffe Entertainment Centre. True, it wasn't up to the *Braveheart* standard, but as I realised I wasn't going to fall, my voice didn't go as high as it did when I yelped.

'1986?' I tried to *Braveheart*.

'1987! It wasn't long after that the sod dropped dead.'

Paint dropped onto her hair. Soon she roared at me. Laughing. I was hanging in the air laughing.

And I sat beside her in her hospital room and saw her life ebbing away.

It is something to see the woman who gave birth to you, held you as an infant, helped make you what you have become, scared. Scared. I had never seen that look before in her eyes.

She looked at me and said, 'I don't think I'm going to get out of here.'

I remembered all the times she had held me and shushed my fears away. Of the cowboy's smoko and banana-and-sugar sandwiches. And now she looked at me and I didn't know what to say. I held her hand and she closed her eyes. But she saw me, saw me not knowing what to do. I think she knew that none of her children knew what to do or what to say, so she did what she always did; she put on a show.

She decided to forgo all her treatments. It wasn't a matter of giving up, she said, but simply coming to understand what was what. 'It's just time to go, that's all, time for bye-byes.' She was definite. No more blessings from Father Brian, the harried hospital priest, whom she called the Bookie because he gave a 'blessing like a bookmaker going through his numbers after a bad day at the Doomben Races'.

The Sisters of Mercy were good because they'd just sit and chat, and the Welsh chaplin was welcome because he and my mother would talk gently in Welsh and she would smile softly as she listened to the language of her youth.

When the palliative-care doctor spoke to her she was clear; she wanted to go.

For some reason, later, when we children gathered in a small room to talk to the palliative-care doctor, he became, somehow and in some silly magical way, Dr Cornel Wilde. Apparently my mother had told Laurie that this particular doctor had nice eyes, like Cornel Wilde, the 'on no accounts' cowboy.

'He's all right,' my mother had said. 'He means well. Not his fault he looks like Cornel Wilde.'

Inspired by this new christening, I went home and Googled Mr Wilde. On the screen appeared a mercilessly funny motion-picture image of a pleasant but silly looking fellow with a pencil-thin moustache and the baggiest, saggiest pair of Robin Hood Lincoln green tights ever worn. The subsequent effect was that when this fine and sensitive doctor spoke to us in kindly tones, one or two of us and sometimes all would giggle. The fact that he looked nothing like Cornel Wilde made it even funnier.

He called us into Mum's room and asked the same question in ten different ways, all in the same solicitous and considerate tone.

'Iris, I know it's hard, I know I've asked many questions,' this kindly man said, 'but one last thing: Is there anything, no matter how big or small, is there anything else that is causing you distress?'

'Yes,' my mother rasped in a painful whisper. 'A little thing. A tiny little thing.'

'What?' asked the doctor. 'What little thing?'

After a moment my mother replied with impeccable timing, 'Tony bloody Abbott.'

The doctor stared, and this brave, eccentric woman said softly, 'Not to worry, son, everything is okey-dokey, it's just time to go.' And she gave him a trembling thumbs-up.

I nearly fell through the floor with laughter. And from what I know of him Tony Abbott would have taken that as a compliment.

Then, as she was given a sedative, we spoke to her about nothing, really. What do you talk about? Somehow the conversation got round to one of her great loves: the players of the Redcliffe Dolphins rugby league teams of the seventies. A bunch of ratbag suburban footy stars from an almost forgotten competition. She would smile at the names and give the same trembling thumbs-up. Names you don't hear much any more. Bevan Bleakley. Ian Thinee. Tony Obst. Bunny Pearce. Peter Leis. Peter Leis the big dairy farmer from the hills around Petrie, he got two thumbs-up. And then she slept.

She woke up when we were all there. We stared at her and she stared at us.

'We're still here, Mum,' said one of my sisters.

'Yes, that's all right for you lot, but what the bloody hell am I still doing here?' she almost roared. She closed her eyes again and we fell about laughing.

The last time I saw her awake was when she opened her eyes, looked at us and smiled and then … And then, of all things, she sang a song, 'You Must Have Been a Beautiful Baby', all the way through. At the end, as she lay in her bed, she gave a shimmy and a shake with her shoulders, smiled, closed her eyes again and slept.

It was impossible not to love her. Oh, she wasn't perfect, but that of course is the glory of a human life. She could be prickly, quick to judge and was sometimes acutely shy and became terribly abrupt about being embarrassed by it. But as she lay there we saw that hers was a life that touched people. Not just us, but her carers. Various nurses would come to hold her hand. Some had been moved to other wards but wanted to say goodbye.

A young doctor popped in. 'We try to look after everyone,' she said, 'but it's hard not to have our favourites.'

For some reason I couldn't understand, she placed an orange – an orange that had been cut into pieces – on my mother's bedside table as if it were a gift. It became clear to us then that Mum was treated not only as a patient but also as a friend.

Cliffy, a big chatty wards man, popped in with a small plastic cup of jelly. 'I know she won't eat it, but I couldn't bear her not having something. She loved her jelly.' He placed the plastic cup gently on her table as if it were a diamond.

And Mary the cleaner came and held my mother's hand and stroked her cheek and said softly, 'Goodbye, darlin', goodbye.'

At her funeral all her children spoke. Corby told a ripping story of how one wet winter's morning she and Rhian were given a lift to school in a deeply useless International truck that was my father's. It had no windscreen – my father kept forgetting to repair it – and had decided because of the weather to take the Holden instead. This left Mum and my sisters in the International. As rain sheeted in, my mother said she'd go as fast as she could, which was on this occasion very fast.

Roaring through the rain she yelled to her daughters, 'It doesn't matter so much when you scream!'

So all three of them howled liked banshees. Soon, Corby said, they were laughing themselves silly. Our mother, putting on a show.

At the end of my mother's funeral her casket was carried away to the tune of 'You Must Have Been a Beautiful Baby'.

As I walked down the aisle I saw some of the mourners: her trivia club friends, some folks from the show society and her Tai Chi master, Wayne. Mayor Allan Sutherland and Ray Frawley, a former mayor, nodded to me from their pews. Both were – as my mum would put it – 'bloody Tories', but were always regarded with friendship and respect.

'They just see the world a little differently and who's to say they're wrong or we're right? Good people are good people,' was my mother's opinion.

Ray Frawley added a little wave and whispered, 'So long, Iris, travel well.'

I thought how genuine acknowledgement of worth and respect is quite rare in today's world of huffing and puffing and political pantomime.

And in the last row was a face I remembered from years ago. His hair was grey but he still looked like he could run through three Fortitude Valley Diehards to score in the corner. Dairy farmer Peter Leis, the centre three-quarter, who was a two thumbs-up Dolphin from the seventies. He nodded.

'Thought I should come. Knew your mum loved the footy.'

The people of her town had come to say, I suppose, that my mum had mattered. And that was something.

———————————————————————————————————————

Six months after my mother's funeral, back in the town where I grew up, I walked along an overcast drizzly beach, the sun shooting through here and there. Suddenly the rain got heavier so I stepped off the beach and took cover under a verandah at my first school. Standing listening to the rain I remembered little school. How big the school had seemed to me when playing Tiggy, how we all thought we were miles away from the teachers. They were, of course, right on top of us, seeing everything. I remembered the smell of the tuck shop and how my mother would help out there every second Wednesday, waving her arms, shouting, putting on a show. Kids would call her the Noisy Mum. The tuck shop used to serve cut oranges, and my mother would hand them out, laughing and yelling at some of the kids.

'Oranges,' she said, 'have such a happy smell. Happy! Smell!' And the kids laughed.

I thought again about the doctor popping an orange by my mother's hospital bed. Almost every time I went to my mother's room near the end of her life, there was a small plate of cut orange on the bedside cabinet.

I looked out across the playground. I supposed the doctor had put it there. A happy smell.

I swore softly to myself with the realisation of that small kindness, something I hadn't been able to understand at the time, even though I'd noticed it. A simple kindness. I took a deep breath and smelt the rain. Then I walked out through that rain, back to the beach among a crowd of seagulls gathered on the sand in a clump, their feathers not uncomfortably ruffling in the wind. And a heron, long and white, waltzed to and fro, treading softly through the flowers and the grass at the sand's edge.

My mother had always said herons bring luck. And if they didn't, then at least you'd seen something lovely so it didn't really matter.

I laughed a little at the logic and then, of all things, I smelt oranges. A giggling little girl walked past with her hand in her mum's, sucking on an orange and jumping in the puddles.

I jumped into the sea. It was cold. I splashed and swam and felt okay. I lay on my back in the grey water and above me the heron floated in the sky. I hummed 'You Must Have Been a Beautiful Baby'.

I thought, Good on you, Mum. She was dead but wasn't really gone. Maybe nobody ever really is, we carry a little of everybody with us. My mother must have been a beautiful baby because she was, all in all, a beautiful human being.

Away from Home
William

You reach a point in life when admitting that you are not good at something doesn't mean that you are giving up – it is just a statement of the bloody obvious. Packing the car – or rather my inability to do just that – is one of those statements.

Packing a car for a family holiday is one of those rituals that happens a couple of times a year and doesn't ever get any easier. We have chugged off in a variety of cars so bound in string, rope and various other fastenings that each time the cars have resembled a giant form of string thing on four wheels.

String things were a particular form of craft that was popular in the 1970s, along with Erich von Däniken's *Chariots of the Gods* and beaten copper. They were pieces of particle board with nails hammered into them and then the added delight of different coloured strands of cotton wound through and around the nails to create a vibrant image. Basically, they were just messy straggly stringy *things*, so our four-wheeled versions were simply string things on an epic scale.

The little ability I have in spatial management is almost nullified by Sarah's love of a challenge. She has stuffed so much gear into various parts of cars that her gift borders on a compulsive disorder. Like some ancient survivalist hunter who leaves no part of their prey unused, so it is with any cavity within the car; it must not go unpacked. And when we finally set off to wherever it is we are going, it's a little like those old documentary films about early space exploration, where the astronauts somehow manage to cram the bulk of their bodies into the tiny confines of their capsules.

I tried to compliment Sarah once on her packing abilities by saying I thought they were so extreme that she reminded me of a participant on a Guinness World Records television show.

She stared at me.

I thought perhaps she wasn't familiar with the show.

'You know, with those muscle-builders who are firemen who try to blow up hot-water bottles like balloons? They've got little heads and massive bodies and they all wear bad jeans and tiny T-shirts. Did you ever see that one?'

'What do you mean? What are you saying?'

Somebody should have stopped me but nobody did. I walked straight into it.

'You know, they've got a gift and they're driven and it's just a bit odd … You know?'

Obviously she didn't.

'It'd help if you took on a little more organising of the car sometimes,' she said.

Organising the car. So many journeys in our string things have been made more of an adventure by my attempts to organise the car. Take the kayaks. The dear old kayaks. Just the thing a family needs to take wherever they may be heading. I decided we needed kayaks, because the family that kayaks together stays together. So I duly bought three of the biggest and most unwieldy kayaks known to humanity and it was my job to tie them to the roof of the various string things that we've owned.

It is on these occasions that Clem tries to make himself scarce. I can't blame him.

'Clem, give us a hand with the kayaks! It's kayak time!' I yell.

Stella has been heard to cry, 'Oh, not the kayaks!'

It's like a catchphrase from an old sitcom where the kayaks are some unwanted neighbours from across the way, Marvin and Gloria Kayak, always dropping in at the most inappropriate times. Maybe something with John Goodman in it.

'Hey, it's Marv and Gloria!'

'Oh no, not the Kayaks!'

Cue laughter.

I tried to christen two of the kayaks Marv and Gloria and maybe call the smallest one Waldo, their son, but it never really stuck.

Clem always manages to do the decent thing in turning up to help his father and also to be given the chance to learn the ancient rope-tying skills that have been passed down from generation to generation of the McInnes family.

Well, not really. The rope-tying made a spectacular departure with my genetic make-up.

Knot. Not. Knot. Not. No knots worth bequeathing. Sadly, I deal only in elegant slipknots that disintegrate with each press of the accelerator.

Clem has a phrase that he drops occasionally: 'Here comes Colin!' in honour of his grandfather, Colin McInnes. Clem never met Col, but he has heard stories my sisters and brother tell; not tales of knot-tying – my old man could tie a knot – but of the old McInnes credo, 'When in doubt, shout.'

Hence the 'Here comes Colin!' cry, because when we drive with those orange prongs on top of the string thing it's only a matter of time before they start to thump on the roof or slide down the bonnet at intersections. Then I yell, 'Those kayaks!'

'Why don't you tie them on properly?'

'It's those kayaks!'

This is cause for some mirth from the back seats and brings on the celebration of the Harrison Ford moment – the moment, christened by Clem, when something goes wrong with the string thing's load and I turn into some character from a bad Harrison Ford film.

One year, while driving a very dear and reliable white Falcon station wagon between the Victorian surf towns of Anglesea and Barwon Heads, a fine kayaking moment took place.

The orange kayaks, secured by me, took off and went into orbit as I hared along the road. The car seemed to lift and suddenly felt quite light as the samba beat of the kayaks upon the string thing's roof ceased abruptly. This should have alerted me, but I was singing along with the radio so it was only when Clem roared, 'Yeah, look at them fly! They're free!' that I saw two tumbling kayaks, Marv and Gloria, soar through the air.

'Kayaks! Kayaks! Kayaks!' was all I could scream. It sounded like some warning of attack, kayaks from outer space. Maybe it gave me a fright. But, you know, when in doubt, shout.

Clem's friend Giancarlo, who was on holiday with us, sort of smiled and did his best not to laugh at the expense of an adult. Clem took care of that. 'Harrison Ford moment!'

I didn't need an introduction, I was on a roll. 'Kayaks! Kayaks!'

I stopped and ran along the road yelling, 'Kayaks! Kayaks!' to any oncoming motorists by way of warning. The only vehicle that came along during my retrieval mission was a little bubble car driven by a pair of old ladies, who crested the hill, slowed, stared and smiled as I yelled at them, 'Kayaks!'

'It's a lovely day,' said one, having wound down the window. She breathed out a long stream of smoke, smiled and flicked out a cigarette butt. Then the pair chugged on their way.

Cradling an orange kayak – Marvin, I think it was – I staggered over and stomped on the butt. This entertained the lads.

I tried to re-tie the kayaks and positioned the boys at various car windows with the especially stupid idea of them holding onto a kayak with one arm curling around the window. All the while I did weird things with my mouth and yelled at nobody.

'Kayaks! Kayaks!' was about the sum total of my conversational ability, but I did manage to find some level of humour with a quote borrowed from one of Harrison's not so fine films, *Air Force One*.

Putting on my best stern-faced Harrison look, I intoned to the kayaks, as Harry did to Gary Oldman, 'Get off my plane!' and later, instead of 'I hate terrorists!' I inserted 'I hate kayaks.'

A reassuring round of chuckles from the kayak-cradlers let me know that all was okay.

These moments of trying to organise, trying to be 'super bloke', pop up time and time again and the more they do the more I learn about life and myself.

One morning I wake up and know it is going to be a particular type of day. I had been deeply asleep, immersed in a log-like slumber. I could have been dreaming but I can't remember. It is the way I wake that is startling. I can't breathe, there is a heavy weight on my chest – a tight constricting weight. I gulp for air and my eyes fight to focus; I can't breathe and when I try to speak I hear only a distant groan.

I try to sit, and struggle in my bed. I shake my head and suddenly I can half see a small smiling face a few centimetres away from mine, blue eyes sparkling. I hear a voice. Actually, I hear a rolling giggle. It is Stella. It all becomes clear.

Well, of course it all becomes clear when my little girl takes her fingers out of my eyes and stops holding my nose. My eyes become a little more attuned to the conscious world and I see Clem sitting behind his sister. She is on my chest so that means he is sinking into my stomach.

Everything starts to compute. Stella and Clem trampolining up and down. Children in our bed, jumping up and down on me, early morning … It's Christmas. No, it's Easter Sunday … No, it's a birthday … No, they're both in here … Oh yes, it's Sunday morning … and we are in a country motel room and I have to get up and deal with the kids.

Sunday morning. Sunday mornings. I used to gently, luxuriantly ease myself into a Sunday morning, like a flower softly unfurling its petals in a slow-motion nature film. Not any more. When you have children things change. And added to that we are in a country motel room because we've stopped overnight on our way to Sydney; we've driven from Melbourne.

I wince at the memory of yesterday. I had tried to take charge of organising things a bit more. It all comes back to me as I stagger inelegantly into and then achingly through the bedroom door out into the lounge area with my children. Yesterday. The string thing we are driving is a nice car. It is a Swedish car. It's old but it goes. It also has those tricks and quirks that some people mark down as character and style.

I filled the tank with petrol at a service station and for some reason decided to check things like the water; organising, taking charge. Why I decided to I don't know, but we were driving a long way and that's what a bloke does – he checks things. Sarah was off buying some Paddle Pops and water and maybe a magazine. She had already checked the tyres before we left, but that didn't mean I couldn't check some other stuff. Yes, blokes check things. Sadly, I am not a complete bloke. That became apparent with my inability to open the bonnet. I stomped and pulled at bits and pieces of the car like a gorilla de-fleaing himself in the zoo. I bumped my head and pressed the horn with my nose three times. The Viking car has a loud horn and I got a fright, so I jumped and bumped my head again and yelled.

My left foot located the bonnet latch by accident, and the mysteries of the Swedish engine were revealed in all their painful glory. Most car bonnets that I open have pretty basic procedures – straight up and you're done. I'm a man at a service station; I know what I'm doing.

I was master of the Viking car. I casually wrenched the bonnet up with a manly flick and it leapt up at my head, slicing through the air like an axe homing in on my chin. It was like a booby trap from a spy film. I screamed and then, not content with an attempted decapitation, the bonnet, with Nordic precision, sheered down. Fearing castration I howled and backed into a man filling his dirt-spattered serious four-wheel drive. I knew he was a serious four-wheel driver because he wore reflective sunglasses and a hat with a bullet belt around the brim. His seriousness doubled when he growled, 'You right?'

I stared and gabbled at him. 'My car, my bonnet. Nearly took my head off … mate.'

My face was distorted in his reflective glasses and I decided to go back to my Viking car. I looked into the depths of a vast array of valves and tubes and shiny stuff. 'I'm checking the water,' I said to no one in particular. I held a water container in my hand but had no idea where to pour its contents. I prodded a few things and caught my finger on something in there, in among all the Viking car's shiny stuff. 'I'm checking the water,' I said again in an effort to convince myself I knew what I was doing.

I stood still for a few moments, as if I were about to take the Viking car by surprise and then I flung my hand back. It worked, my hand plus most of my fingers were free and as my arm jerked back across the engine it banged against a water container, it had a water level on the outside. Success! I knew what I was doing. I was at the service station and I knew what I was doing.

I snapped open the top of the water container, which seemed quite full, and poured in more water. The water overflowed and I snapped the top back on tightly. I nodded to Mr Serious Four-wheel driver and got into the car. Once inside I informed everybody, 'I have checked the water.'

This was exactly what I said about twenty minutes later when the Viking car sat on the side of the road with its bonnet raised to the blue sky in surrender to the elements, overheating.

'We'll just let it stand and cool down.'

To keep the kids occupied I suggested a game of kick-to-kick while we waited for the tow truck to arrive. An incredulous Sarah found this slightly insane as we weren't that far from a highway and our kicking skills weren't that polished. She might have had a point; when I attempted a quick kick on the sly, I managed to land the ball inside the open bonnet. I tried not to make too much noise when I burnt my hand trying to retrieve the ball. We then sat around the steaming Viking playing 'I spy' instead.

'I spy with my little eye something beginning with B,' said Clem.

'Bird?' said Sarah.

'Bush?' said William.

'Branch?' said Stella.

'No,' said Clem. 'Broken car.'

We stopped playing after that. Thankfully the tow truck turned up.

'I checked the water.' That's what I said when the man with the tow truck arrived.

The tow-truck man asked me if I was *sure* I checked the water.

'Of course.'

Sarah asked where I put the water.

I pointed with a cut finger – mangled by all that shiny stuff in the Viking car's engine – to where I put the water.

There was a pause, and then the tow-truck man looked away. Then there was a silence and Sarah slowly asked me if I read what was on top of the container where I put the water. My finger started to hurt.

I read, 'Wiper water only.'

Oh … oh … oh … My finger hurt.

Sunday morning in the motel room and I sit and remember all of this. The children laugh and giggle. I try to shush them. So what if I put radiator water in the wiper-water container? Down the road at the repair shop the Viking car sits on blocks awaiting three days of loving attention from a mechanic, a sizeable chunk of my finger under its nasty bonnet. For three days the hotel room would be our home. And that is okay. We are together.

Who cares, I think, what Mr Serious Four-wheel driver would make of someone who would put radiator water in the wiper-water container? He would probably think that such a man would be the type of bloke who'd be frightened by the prospect of opening the bonnet of a car. Well, he's probably right.

Then, through that early morning fug, I realise that it isn't that I've done something stupid, it's the fact that I pretended to know what I was doing when it was obvious I had no idea. Why didn't I just say, 'Well, I'm not too sure about this. Better find someone who can help me.' Why didn't I do that? Is it a blokey thing? Bloke must know all, can't show ignorance. Some dopey pride factor? What a colossal waste of time. Think of all those men, those blokes throughout history who bumbled along pretending to know what they were doing, not asking for help, not admitting to ignorance or doubt, just pretending. All those empires lost, the course of history changed because these men couldn't find it in them to ask for help.

I lie there and think and realise something else. Children giggling doesn't sound out of place on a Sunday morning, especially when your wife is laughing along right next to you. It's the sort of sound you can float into the day on.

I smile and they giggle. I ask Sarah if she'd like a cup of tea. She nods. I collect the makings and as I grab the kettle her voice floats into the room. 'Make sure you check the water.'

The toilet block was new. It was just outside the road that led straight into Kakadu. It was clean. That was before our family met a cane toad.

We'd driven from Darwin to the national park: Sarah, me, Clem, Stella and Nanna Anna. We drove in a hired string thing and thankfully had no kayaks to tie on the roof. What we did have to put up with, though, was an old friend of mine, the cane toad.

I remember my father sitting at the big table we'd eat around laughing and saying, 'People down south think toads are just a Queensland thing, but it's only a matter of time till the buggers will be everywhere and then we'll see how funny they all think it is.'

Thankfully I live in Melbourne, which is, to my knowledge anyway, cane-toad free.

In the Northern Territory it's a different matter. Ominously at the airport there were signs warning about cane toads. There was even a sign asking people to check their baggage and make sure there were no traces of the dreaded pest. The mind boggles as to why any sane person would want to pack a cane toad in their luggage, but who knows the way accessorising can change.

Sarah, with her ever-present sense of doing the right thing, took it upon herself to make sure that if we saw any cane toads we would try to save the Territory from invasion. I could have told her that the invasion was already well and truly underway and that we should just enjoy the Territory as we found it, but she had a determined look in her eyes so I nodded.

It was when we happened upon the new toilet block that it all went wrong. I saw it first. A whopper. About three or four hamburgers in size sitting by a stump not far from the entrance to the Gentlemen's. The kids were watching Sarah and Nanna Anna gaze for birds and I managed to stifle a shriek and maintain an almost normal walk as I sauntered back to the car.

'You all right?' asked Sarah.

'Sure. Sure.'

'Why is your voice so high?'

'It's not.'

'It is,' said Stella. 'Why is it high?'

'Come on, let's go,' I said, and I knew my voice was high. 'Let's get in the car,' I said and my voice sounded like Darth Vader's.

Sarah laughed and walked towards the toilet. Clem let out a yelp. 'Toad! Toad by the toilets!'

'Let's get in the car!' and my voice was all over the scale.

Anna turned from peering at a parrot and asked, 'What's she found, Will?'

'Toad,' Stella giggled.

We should have got in the car, but there was no hope; Sarah had that look in her eye. She was off to save the Kakadu.

'What are you doing?' I sounded like Michael Jackson.

'We can't let it get into the Kakadu.'

'Oh, for Christ's sake, they're everywhere.'

'Swear jar!' yelled Stella.

'What has she found?'

'Nanna, Mum has found a toad.'

The kids danced like loons, as if it was a festival. A festival of the toad.

Sarah looked around for something. 'Well we can't let this one get into the park. It's a pest. We can't just leave it here.'

I realised she was going to kill it. But she was a novice; she picked up a rock and tried to throw it at the toad invader.

'Oh, look, that's not going to do any good!' It was the tone of the all-knowing middle-aged male that made Sarah give me the look.

'Well, I grew up in Queensland ...' I said slowly.

She threw the rock, hit the toad and the wretched thing puffed itself up like a life jacket self-inflating. Everybody shrieked and the toad bounded into the toilets and I bounded into the car.

Sarah turned to me and I looked up at her. 'Well, I can't go in the Gents and you grew up in Queensland.'

I stared at her and at my children who were doubled over in mirth.

'Dad's going to get the toad!' yelled Clem.

'Toady, toady, toad!' chanted Stella.

Even Anna began to smile at me.

I have a deep-seated dislike of toads that borders on the phobic, and there I sat in our hired string thing, my floral hat pulled down on my head, looking out at the toilet block and my laughing family, knowing a desperado lurked somewhere in some dark corner of the gleaming dunny. It was completely insane, what could I do? And yet that inner bloke, that fearless pioneer spirit stirred within me.

Sarah laughed. Really laughed. When she really laughs she laughs with every inch of her body. 'Your face!' she got out between wheezes.

'Do it for Kakadu, Dad,' said Stella.

I got out of the car and walked into the toilet like Clint Eastwood in *Unforgiven*. Well, actually more like some cousin of Mr Bean's.

It's a hell of a thing to kill a toad, take away all it's got, all it's ever going to have.

Clem cheered me on with words that instilled in me a deep sense that this was completely silly. 'Give it up for the Green Knight!'

This truly was a bad action movie. I peered around the entrance and saw the pumped-up reptile and I shrieked. Then I went into vengeful-protector-of-Kakadu mode and threw anything I could find at that toad. Sometimes I hit it and sometimes the thing dodged my aim like a pinball. I hit the basin, then the trough and then the basin again and finally I put the poor thing out if its misery. Or so I thought.

I heard footsteps and I was sure it would be my thankful family coming to see me, the conqueror of the cane toad. I turned, almost breathless and slightly hysterical, and panted like a gladiator. 'I killed it – the toad is dead. I killed the toad.'

I didn't see any of my family. An old man with steel-framed specs and one of the worst toupees I have ever seen stared at me and spoke in a deep rumbling old man's voice. 'What are you bastards doing in here?'

His eyes were huge behind the specs and his face was smeared with a hint of disgust.

God knows what my efforts at pest control sounded like but this gentleman looked around the toilet, repulsed. Maybe this old bloke thought there was some sort of orgy going on in the toilet block. 'You the only one here?'

I nodded and said like a fool, 'Just the toad and me.'

'The toad?' he looked slightly amazed. 'I thought you were breaking the toilet – you have! You've nearly broken the bloody toilet!' he repeated and held out a gnarled hand.

He looked around to make sure there was nobody else there.

It was at this point I tried to make it clear that I was no vandal but somebody trying to do the right thing.

'I killed the toad.' I pointed towards where I thought the body lay and as I did the poor thing puffed itself up. I reacted like the lion I am and gripped the old fellow's arm and roared, 'It's *alive!*'

Even over the echoes inside the toilet block I could hear Sarah laughing.

The bug-eyed man looked at me, shook my hand off his shirt and muttered, 'You big bloody pansy,' as he limped towards the toad.

I saw him pick it up and thump it on the basin.

And then I ran out of the toilet yelling, 'He killed the toad!'

I turned back to see an old man with high-hitched grey shorts, a floral polo shirt and caramel sandals limping away to a bin with a dangling toad held in his hands by a leg. It looked tiny. And it took hours for my family to stop laughing.

Being away from home doesn't necessarily mean it's always circus time. A day after the toad-in-the-toilet incident we found ourselves on a cruise, drifting through the wetlands of the Kakadu. The guide was a pleasant fellow, who described the wildlife and spoke about the character of the animals, but basically he rated the wildlife by their taste.

'Magpie geese there; beautiful birds, but you've got to cook 'em slow or they'll be as tough as old leather.'

'Now that's a beautiful fish that little Jack, tasty as.'

I was glad Anna couldn't hear up the back.

After a while his words drifted away and we all just sat and floated and gloried at the colour, grace and timelessness of the landscape. It was blissful and, in a very quiet and un-fancy way, incredibly humbling.

It was an intimate journey, and even though there were only a few other people on the boat we shared it together.

That night an old man from America was sitting at the bar in the hotel. He had been on the cruise with his wife and beckoned me over. He was drinking bourbon.

'You were on that boat today, sir?'

'I was.'

'You'd like a drink?'

'Thanks,' I said and asked for bourbon. 'Just to keep you company,' I added.

He smiled. 'You know I'm eighty-four?'

'No. You're doing well.'

He smiled and said I was too kind but he was only going to buy me one drink. 'Out on the boat today, out there on that water, I don't know, it was beautiful.'

'It was.'

'I've seen some things in my life. But out there today, I thought if I was to die, then it was okay because I've lived a life.' He laughed and said sorry.

I told him it was okay.

'I've got a son about your age. I just rang him at home. It's early. I just rang him to say how much I loved him. I don't often do that but that boat trip, it was something. Just wanted to tell him. And I rang our daughter. It was even earlier for her.'

We drank a bit and didn't say much.

'You been to Australia before?'

'During the war, the Second World War.' He laughed and told me he'd been stationed up in New Guinea and how one night they watched a cowboy movie, a John Wayne serial. 'And there was a gunfight, old Duke's shooting away and the bad guys are shooting back at him and I thought, Christ in hell, those shots are loud! And all of a sudden the Japanese were shooting back at the screen. Sons of bitches were shooting at the cloth screen. They hit the Duke but he kept on riding. Damndest thing. We scattered and I remember thinking that John Wayne wears a lot of lipstick for a cowboy.'

We finished our drinks and I asked him if he'd like another bourbon.

He shook his head. He got up from the bar and shook my hand. 'Have a good life, son, and hold your kids close when you can. Just remember to tell them what you think of them when you can.' He walked away like an old man. A long way from home and yet as close to his family as he could be.

Later, when we left, I checked my bill and saw that I had bought two bourbons at the bar. The old bugger hadn't bought me one at all. But I laughed. Why not? He was away from home.

One of the great joys of being away from home is returning and telling your neighbourhood all about your whole adventure. And sometimes just a quick meeting unlocks all sorts of memories from a trip.

I thought about my barber and the time I met Buzz Aldrin when I was on holidays.

He – the barber not Buzz Aldrin – chats to me about the moon landing as I sit in the barber's chair. It is coming up to the fortieth anniversary.

The barber had watched it at the time with his parents and his uncle. 'Forty years ago, a lot can happen, mate,' says the barber. 'I never thought I'd be cutting hair. A lot can happen. Just look at him.' The barber points to an old man standing outside, smoking like a chimney. 'That's my uncle, he was our age once.'

I look at the uncle, and he does look very old.

'They've told him to hold back on the smokes and the booze but he sinks the piss like there's no tomorrow,' says the barber.

What a great phrase, 'sinks the piss like there's no tomorrow'.

The barber remembers watching the moon landing and all the other stuff the astronauts did. 'My uncle, he didn't believe any of it. "Bullshit – bullshit!" he said. "There is no wind on the moon, why is the flag waving? Footprints everywhere?"'

The uncle likes a conspiracy.

'"They're not up there!" Typical European, mate, he thought there was a conspiracy when the car started on a cold morning,' laughs the barber.

I watched the moon landing at school, jammed into the music room. The music teacher said, 'The world has changed forever.'

I got bored quickly and went home hoping something else was on Channel 0 in Brisbane, after I had been told the world had changed forever. I watched the back end of 'George of the Jungle' and a television serial about the Seventh Cavalry charging around with big gloves and a fluttering flag. The afternoon seemed to follow a pattern: waving American flags.

'But there's no wind on the moon,' said the uncle.

My father believed, shaking his head and looking at the moon shining over the bay that night. 'They're up there, up there … Bugger me.'

'Bugger me' was the highest expression of awe and wonder he could muster.

And later, over ice-cream and pineapple – a treat to celebrate the world changing forever – my father added, 'Well done, Yanks. Although they never would have got off the ground if it hadn't been for Jerry.'

I had no idea what he meant but later my mother told me, when she tucked me into bed, it was the Germans whom the Americans had to thank. The scientists the Americans caught at the end of the war were smarter than the ones the Communists caught.

The war, the war. Back then 'the war' meant only one conceivable conflict – not the Vietnam War; well, that was just a conflict. The Second World War, when people knew what they were fighting for, when good and bad were clear. People fought the good war, the certain war.

The men in the chubby white suits were named Buzz and Neil – 'American names'. They sounded funny.

'So American,' said my mother, and added, 'at least Kennedy would be happy.'

John F. Kennedy had said by the end of the decade that America would send men to the moon. It must have sounded like just another speech. But they got there, though

Kennedy, of course, wasn't around to see it, becoming a major conspiracy-theory industry himself, even more so than the moon landing. Although the barber's uncle loves the moon conspiracy, J.F.K.'s turns more coin.

'And old Kennedy started it all,' says the barber. 'He was looking at the moon when he should have been looking at the grassy knoll. Should've looked there, mate!'

The astronauts were all alike, it seemed. Neat, white, intelligent-seeming men with buzz-cuts and steady gazes.

A lot can happen in forty years.

Armstrong became a very rich and humble recluse. Buzz Aldrin, the second man on the moon, was a little more operatic. Depression and alcohol abuse plagued him. He openly and bravely spoke about his problems and then began his life again as a motivational speaker, among other things. Hungover once, I sat in a hotel watching morning television and out of nowhere popped Buzz in a space-style tracksuit on some bizarre walking contraption. An exercise machine.

He smiled as he wobbled away.

'The moon-walker – it's the best walk I have had since the moon.'

I laughed quite a lot.

Nixon welcomed the astronauts home and spoke to them via telephone. He was a president who had more problems and twists to his mind and character than Buzz Aldrin could ever have known, and Nixon never went to the moon. Well, Nixon's not around anymore. A lot can happen in forty years.

Those pleasant-looking white Americans would go again to the White House and meet another president. An African American.

Just ten months before Neil and Buzz waddled around on the moon, Martin Luther King had been murdered in public. Civil rights and equality were looked on with suspicion and fear.

I tell the barber I met Buzz Aldrin once.

'Get away,' he says.

'Yes. I did.'

It was in Hollywood, of all places, where I was mixing work with a holiday with

Clem. We went to a screening of Sarah's film *Look Both Ways* at Paramount Studios. Sarah, showing commendable priorities, stayed home in Australia, preferring surfing lessons with Stella on the south coast to tripping the bright lights of LA. At the party in the foyer afterwards, people mingled and bingled in the manner they usually do at such events, when a very pleasant former deputy prime minister of Australia appeared from the crowd, towing an old man with a level gaze.

'William, may I introduce to you Colonel Buzz Aldrin, the second man to step on the face of the moon.'

Buzz shook my hand. 'That was a pretty good movie,' he said, 'but you should make more movies like *The Dish*.'

'You think?'

'Yeah, I do.'

'What about *Apollo 13*?'

'Oh, that was great.'

Space movies. Buzz liked space movies. I tried to think of any I knew.

'*Marooned*,' I said.

'With Gregory Peck. Oh yeah!' said Buzz. 'And Richard Crenna floated off into space – what a way to go!'

I ran out of space movies and so grabbed Clem. He came over and said how big the soft drinks were here and that somebody who looked like Peter Costello was laughing with him about it. I introduced him to Colonel Buzz Aldrin.

'Who?' said my son in his then-little voice. 'Who is this man?'

'This is Buzz Aldrin, the second man to walk on the moon!'

'The moon?' Clem stared at him.

'The moon!' said the nice former deputy prime minister and laughed. 'That's right, the one in the sky. He was the second man on the moon.'

Buzz smiled and posed for a photo with Clem and as he smiled my son asked, 'Where's the first man on the moon?'

'Well, sonny, the old bastard isn't anywhere near here.' Buzz turned and disappeared back into the crowd.

I don't tell the barber that, but I tell him I met Buzz Aldrin when I was on holiday with my son. Mixing a bit of business with pleasure.

'Get away,' says the barber again and nods to his uncle. 'Hey, Uncle, Bill met one of those blokes who walked on the moon.'

The old man stares at me. 'Bullshit! Moon? Bullshit.'

A lot can happen in forty years, but some things stay the same.

I know it's the school holidays when certain things are noted. Just like the turn of the seasons, things happen: a leaf falling, the first frost on the ground or, in the case of school holidays, I fully comprehend what has become of me when I find myself on the Gold Coast and hear Sarah say, 'You are not wearing them. You can't wear them.'

Wear what?

'Not even Vaughan is wearing them!'

I waddle out from the change rooms of a water theme park on the Gold Coast with my middle-aged indulgence barely covered in my Speedos. Or perhaps it would be more apt to say that my Speedos were almost completely covered by my middle-aged indulgence. While I was trying to mould myself into them I thought for a moment that with a bit of creative gut-sucking I might be able to get away with them. These are essential skills that any out-of-condition or going-to-seed actor is well-acquainted with. Thirty years ago I might have got away with it but no, not today.

Clem looks at me with a mixture of pity and deep concern. 'You are not trying to do your Mario Milano thing are you?' he mutters.

He has never seen Mario Milano, but when he was much younger I used to entertain him at swimming lessons with my high-hitched impersonations of the great wrestling hero of my childhood. I laugh and grip the top of my Speedos.

'Oh, Dad, don't,' he says and laughs.

Vaughan ambles up in a ballooning rash vest and boardies.

'Bill,' he says in his best big-brother tone. 'What you are wearing is a crime against humanity. Sometimes, mate, it pays not to advertise.'

Even the most self-deluded ham knows that he must accept the point made. Not that many seem to be wearing them. There are fellow travellers, but they are invariably the kind of buffed, close-eyed European breed with tightly cropped hair who wear funny sandals. One even has socks with his Dr Scholl's and fire-engine red budgie smugglers. One of them stares at me.

'Yes,' I say to Vaughan. 'You're right.'

I make a furtive dash to the theme-park shop and there find a group of brethren. Porky, blank-gazed men about my age are huddled around a stand selling more appropriate attire for the activities of the park. Baggy black shorts.

'One size fits all!' says another of our band breathlessly.

Suitably clothed I embark upon a day at the theme park. We are holidaying again with Vaughan's family.

Sooner or later thousands of people like us seem to find themselves heading to this part of Australia for a school-holiday break. Usually it is the winter break. And usually it's the Gold Coast. It is Australia's very own corner of Disney-style 'worlds' – a strip of theme parks and resorts that are designed to make holidays easier. The land of the tourist dollar. The land of unbridled development and pursuit of that dollar. And school holidays are the pinnacle of that pursuit.

It is too easy to poke fun at such a place and mock the people who flock there. And to be honest, I have been to some pretty dreadful places for an organised 'holiday': an island on the Great Barrier Reef that featured a 'unique nature night walk', hosted by a wildlife guide who spent most of the time uninterestedly flicking at things in the dark while informing the stupefied gaggle of holiday-makers about how his marriage had collapsed and his life had hit an all-time low.

It was on this island we holidayed with Vaughan and Sue and their three kids, and if one McInnes can be a circus on display then two McInneses are Barnum & Bailey's big top.

The island had an entertainment team who were supposed to organise activities for the guests, but there was no real need for any assistance when Vaughan tried to organise the kids at breakfast. To say we were loud is an understatement. Sarah and Sue wouldn't come out for brekkie until we had gone.

There were louder people, I suppose, but none who sang songs to their breakfasts like Vaughan, especially his one of longing dedicated to hash browns. He sang this to the tune of *Exodus*:

'*This hash brown is mine,*
God gave this hash brown to me.'

Singing was a part of the wonder of that particular holiday, because we stumbled across a man playing an electronic organ and singing along in the bar at night. He was so amazingly bad that we fell in love with him. He winced as he sang and occasionally shook his head in slight amazement at how far he had been from the note he had tried to hit. He sweated a lot and had trouble coordinating his hands and organ-playing with his singing. Best of all he specialised in Chris de Burgh songs and he looked remarkably like Tony Obst, a former fullback for the Redcliffe Dolphins, so he was instantly christened Tony or Obsty by Vaughan and me.

We sat almost every night in the bar and listened to him nearly strangle himself singing 'The Lady in Red' and the truly epic 'Don't Pay the Ferryman', when he swallowed not one but two bugs during the one song.

'This guy is a genius,' Vaughan declared.

Amazingly, our families holidayed together on another island in the Whitsundays a couple of years later.

Sarah and Sue were going to disappear, do a few day trips to escape the McInnes boys and perhaps experiment with cocktails and daiquiris, but the morning we arrived Sarah discovered she was pregnant with Stella and so for her it became a very low-key affair.

For Vaughan our happy news was reason to celebrate, and he ran back from the bar with some even greater news. 'Obsty is singing and he's just as bad as ever!'

The two of us sat at the master's feet and listened to him sing the same songs. We gave him a standing ovation when he swallowed a bug during one of his songs. True, it wasn't 'Don't Pay the Ferryman', but he came close to immortality when a moth the size of a small plane disappeared into his throat while he warbled with wobbly note control, 'I Just Called to Say I Love You'.

'This guy is *pure* genius.'

It was during that night that Vaughan decided we should go water skiing. 'We should recreate the Timex ad from the seventies, when that bloke had the watch on his foot and held it up for the camera.'

I nodded, having no idea what he was talking about, but he was my big brother and we were on holiday, so the next day we went water skiing. This meant Vaughan sat in the back of the boat with a drink, urging the driver to go full bore for Mr Timex.

'He likes it fast, mate, let him have it!'

I had no idea how to water ski, but armed with a massive hangover and little ability I was dragged along behind the boat for an hour.

Vaughan sat, heaving with laughter as I lost control of the rope and finally my shorts. I was, he said, like a cat in a washing machine.

'Lose you dacks again, Bill, it's up there with Obsty swallowing the fly!'

And to top it off, Vaughan sat in the back chortling as I 'Dambuster-ed' like the old 1950s war film about bombers that dropped great bouncing bombs against dams in the Ruhr.

He wore a straw hat and saluted with a clenched fist, yelling with all his might, 'Dambusters!'

My bouncing bombs were bounced so much I couldn't walk straight for a week.

School holidays. There will always be organisation that crumbles and bookings that go west and deals that are invariably better when you read about them in the colourful brochures. These things are a part of life. But what is also a part of life is that unique wonderfulness when moments are just fun.

And you never know where you will find them.

Sometimes in a theme park that sells baggy black shorts to cover the sartorial mistakes of an over-indulged middle-age man. For a place that is so attuned to being body conscious, this theme park on the Gold Coast is an oasis of acceptance and commonality. All shapes and sizes heave and run and shout around that complex, swept along by the elemental joy of water. It is a lot of daggy fun.

It's the school holidays and families and friends and strangers all shriek and laugh together. It's that elemental frolicking in water and being taken out of yourself that makes a day out. It is the magic of water. Body shape doesn't seem to matter. Pretty young bodies don't primp and pose and pout, and there's no time for embarrassment if you're not a living sculpture – we are all running too fast to get to the next silly water adventure. Running with the short and lumpy, awkward and skinny. People. People all haring about together having fun.

I heave along with my giggling children and feel that joy of skittering across wet concrete by a pool, feeling the hardness beneath my feet, shivering a little and flicking water beads at my kids. The years slip away and I crash headlong with the sensations of my childhood, while I share those of my children.

On something called the Mammoth River Plunge I ride with Vaughan and he turns to me with real fear in his eyes and screams, 'Mate! Mate, big people shouldn't go on this!'

We ride to the lip of the fibreglass tube and both of us bellow like mad bulls.

At the end of the ride a young attendant laughs easily and says we should go again, because we two brothers are such a good advertisement for the Mammoth River Plunge.

'Piss off!' is all we can muster.

As we recover our kids come roaring around and we stagger back in line for the Mammoth River Plunge. Again.

'We haven't seen it this wet since 1951. Yeah, wettest July since 1951.'

That is what the guy in the pub with the pale eyes said.

I wasn't that surprised. Sarah has a drought-breaking spirit. Anywhere we go it rains. When it's time to board a plane the blue skies suddenly turn bilious black and open up. In Broome she outdid herself; it poured for more than half the holiday, and when it rains in Broome it's sort of exciting because it buckets. But continuous bucketing does dampen the spirits, not so much of we tourists but of the people who run the shops and services in the northern town. They were so anxious to make as much money as they could from the streams of visitors that their displeasure at the rain bled into disaffection with the wider world.

It was a tourist town and this was one of the peak seasons, so Stella bumped into a friend from Melbourne on Cable Beach. She told us, 'You know, not even the camel rides on the beach were operating earlier in the week. I mean, what's Broome with no camel rides?'

Well, there was always the World Cup or even the football, whatever code you followed. Most people staying at Cable Beach like us piled into the Divers Tavern, a big suburban-looking beer barn on one of the most isolated parts of the Australian coastline.

It was a mix all right, the crowd at the Divers. Because of the World Cup there were national strips from all over the world. A tall man in a Dutch shirt was standing at the bar, where there were also Argentinian and Spanish and German versions. A woman in a German shirt was looking up at the AFL on one of the television monitors.

'I like the way they look, these men.'

Clem took the moment to barrack for the Dogs.

'Go the Dogs!' he said to her. 'Go the Dogs!'

She smiled. 'Okay, go the Dogs!'

It was then that the fellow with the pale eyes spoke to me. He'd been staring at me for some time. I was over at the tavern to watch a bit of the World Cup soccer or any code that caught my fancy. Clem and his cousin James had wanted to come over to watch a game between Germany and Argentina, but we had to wait a bit so Clem was forced to put up with watching Hawthorn just pip his beloved Western Bulldogs. He already knew the result as he'd been informed via James's iPhone over dinner.

'Never know, Clem,' said James, 'they might win this one on the telly.'

Clem smiled and then shook his head as he stood next to the happiest and loudest Hawthorn supporter in Broome.

'Go Hawkers!' the man cried.

Clem just shook his head again. James laughed. 'There's always the rugby, Clem.'

And that was when I saw him. The pale-eyed man. A smooth-faced, short-haired fellow wearing Cowboys rugby league shorts and thongs, a T-shirt and holding a can of Emu Export. He was staring at me and then sidled over.

He nodded a few times and we had a grunted conversation about the footy.

'Those Broncs, they come good, even without the Origin boys.'

I nodded.

He introduced himself. He said his name. I didn't hear it. So I called him 'mate'.

I took a stab and called him Trent. He looked like a Trent.

He looked at me and yelled, 'Dion!'

'Dion. Sorry, mate.'

He shrugged his shoulders. 'That's all right. You that actor bloke?'

Both James and Clem were looking on. I said I am.

'Thought so.'

I offered to buy him a drink and he accepted. I got two Emu Export Bitters.

'You and me must be the only c---- drinking Emu. It's a blackfella's beer up here.'

I told him I used to like it when I was at drama school in Perth.

He looked at me and I knew who he reminded me of: one of those faces from those black-and-white photos of old diggers or early settlers with their light eyes and stretched skin. A bit blank looking.

'What are you up to … mate … Dion?' I asked.

'Just sinking the piss on a Friday night like most blokes do.'

'Fair enough,' I said, 'but what are you doing in Broome?'

'Work in earth-moving, driving a grader.'

I nodded. There was a pause and the Broncos scored a try.

'Them Broncos, coming good,' said Dion.

The Hawks got a goal after the Doggies fumble. The Hawker cried in delight. Clem shrugged and he and James looked on at Dion and me.

'Used to be a shearer, ended up in Broome learning a new trade and, mate, I fucking loves it. Not a local, eh? Born in Wollongong, place called Dapto.'

'I know Dapto!' I cried, 'The Dapto Dogs.'

Dion nodded. Sort of impressed.

'And there was an old Shell servo. I bought a packet of Winnie Reds there once.'

Now he was impressed.

I remember it; I was driving with Sarah in her old S-series Valiant just after we met. That summer we were deciding whether or not what we were doing was just a fling or something more serious.

I wondered now, in this beer barn in Broome, what I had thought our relationship would be. I didn't think it would have led me to this night, nearly twenty-two years later with my seventeen-year-old son staring at me talking to Dion, me and him drinking 'blackfellas' beer'.

'I liked Dapto,' I said for no reason other than I liked thinking of how Sarah drove into that servo with Dwight Yoakam blaring out of her tape deck and smiling at me.

'Dapto. Dapto's shit, mate,' said Dion. 'Broome is where it's at. I'm working with great people, they're teaching me stuff and I'm learning heaps. Six days a week I work. And I can tell you it's better than shearing. Did that for a bit. Mate, I'll get my grader's licence and then I can live on them big beef properties. Do the grading. Got me missus up here with me and we've got a kid. It's sweet.' He took a swig of his Emu. 'She wanted to stay in Port Hedland, but it was an arsehole of a place. Broome is where it's at, mate.' He drained the Emu.

'Day off tomorrow?

'No, start at five-thirty in the morning.'

That was not that far away. I winced a bit and Clem still looked over. I wondered what he thought.

'What do you reckon about the gas plant they want to build up here?' Dion suddenly asked me.

I told him I thought it was good for Australia. More money, more jobs.

'I hope they don't fuck it up, I like it the way it is. The Abos want it, you know. They want the money. I hope they don't fuck it up; it's a perfect place. Beautiful. Hope the blackfellas know what they're doing.' He burped and shook his can at me. 'Anothery?'

'Think I'll be right, Dion.'

'Fuck that, mate; you can't squib me on a shout.'

I nodded. It was like I was talking to someone from another era. He was all of twenty-three, yet he sounded like something from a Chips Rafferty film. Or maybe not. Maybe that's what some men are like.

I looked at Clem. He smiled.

I glanced around the pub and over in a corner there was a bit of argy-bargy going on. A big bouncer walked over and pushed a few people. Young men, maybe James's age, around twenty, pushed and shoved. They had funny pointed haircuts and tight jeans with baggy crotches. Definitely out-of-towners. But they pushed and shoved like young men everywhere with too much grog in them tend to do. It was loud and the boys were tired, James couldn't hear the commentary so we decided to go back to our unit.

First I had to deal with Dion's shout. I did so. I nodded my thanks.

He stared at me and then nodded.

I nodded again.

He nodded and said, 'Be seeing you then.'

'Yeah,' I said.

We walked out and the German girl yelled at Clem, '*Go Dogs!*'

Clem smiled and said, 'Bulldogs go international.'

The unit was not far but the fresh air killed the noise of the tavern almost dead. It was warm, but still raining. A young woman vomited in the corner of the car park while a young man held her bag. She said 'Thank you' very politely and then vomited again.

I thought of Clem. He was seventeen. He was taller than me. Bigger than me. Stronger than me. My little boy, who I cradled in the tiny room at the hospital when he was born.

'That bloke – Dion. What did you think of him?' I asked.

'Did you know him, Will?' asked James.

'No, I don't know him, mate. He's just some bloke.'

We walked for a bit.

'What did you think of him, Clem?'

Clem said nothing for a few paces.

'He's just.'

He stopped and I said, 'He's just what?'

'He's just a man getting drunk. Saying stuff he probably doesn't talk about that much. Stuff that sounds wrong, but stuff he thinks he can talk about. He's just a man.'

I looked across at Clem. He still looked young, younger than his years, maybe, but I suddenly felt happiness inside. Happiness that what Sarah and I started all those years ago wasn't just a summer fling.

It was further south in Western Australia a few years earlier when I found myself away from home, in Busselton on a book tour. I was driving from Perth to Margaret River with a pleasant Irish sales rep. She'd asked me if I'd like to stop anywhere on the way and I had said I'd like to see the Busselton jetty.

Years before I had walked along it when I was at drama school. It was a pencil-thin arc of timber that curled out over the sea for what seemed like an eternity.

The sales rep said it was far too windy for her so she'd wait in the car. I nodded and told her I'd just wander out along the jetty and wouldn't be that long. She gave me the thumbs-up and I was off.

It was windy and the sea was up. Rain spat a bit and stung my face as I walked. It felt good to be out there on the boards.

I've always liked jetties, always. You walk along them, usually dawdling, just taking in the view, just wandering along. Sometimes you'll look ahead and see the end, but usually it's a gradual completion. You're prepared for the end when it comes.

I used to think life was a bit like a jetty. One step after another, wandering along enjoying the view and then, sometimes before you can even appreciate it, the walk finishes. What seemed like a vast distance was only a trick of the water. It makes things seem longer than they are and sometimes, even though you know it's a deception, you let yourself believe the lie anyway.

The waves were up and the foam white. I liked the way this jetty curved out and around, it didn't just shoot straight out ahead. Yes, I liked this jetty.

I was away from home and on my own, my family was on the other side of the country. I thought of a jetty in Tathra on the New South Wales coast that was about three or four metres above the water.

One summer afternoon Clem and Stella and I stood on that jetty and watched a father and son leap into the air and fall into the water with a whoop. They had done this every year for ten years and always took a photograph before the leap.

Ten years.

We decided, the three of us, to jump in and bomb off the jetty. I used to do that off the Redcliffe jetty as a boy, but it didn't seem this high. That's what I said to Sarah, who was in her preferred role of chronicler of all things holiday and trying to capture the moment on camera.

I finally managed to jump and that emptying rush from my guts came back and the next minute I plunged into the deep blue water. I flapped to the top and, just like every other person leaping, let out a huge whoop.

Stella laughed with her whole body, just like her mother. And fell, laughing, into Sarah's arms.

I stood on the Busselton jetty and looked out across the sea. It was up, churning. Green water oiling up against itself and then smashing into the pylons. I walked on and thought of the jetty at Queenscliff. It was there one night that Sarah and I scattered the ashes of our first child, Cosmo. It was cold and the walk to the end seemed to take forever. We paused for a bit at the end of the jetty and stood under the fluorescent light. Sarah made a small sound and held my hand. 'It'll be too cold for him.'

I held her.

When she gave birth to him, when she knew he'd never breathe, the look on her face was the most beautiful I had ever seen. She was so happy. And she held her precious boy close to her. It was the saddest thing I have seen yet also the most beautiful.

I looked at the waves and suddenly thought that we could have blamed somebody if we were different people. I wondered why we had never really blamed anybody.

I had held him not long after. He was warm and salty. They put him in a room deep in the hospital. A cold room. I went a couple of times. And, once, so did my sister Rhian. She asked me if she could come. I said, 'Of course.'

'I'd like to hold my nephew,' she had said.

I thought of Rhian now, on the Busselton jetty. I thought of just how much it meant to me that she had held my son, that she had wanted to cuddle her nephew.

The sea was up and rolling and the rain still stung my face.

I was away from home, standing out on a curling finger of wood over the water and I looked down to see plaques fastened onto the boards. They were plaques of remembrance to people whose ashes had been scattered into the water below. Simple words, boldly engraved on the brass plates, but in the wind and rain they read with a beauty that moved me.

A man of great pride
Who left a lasting impression
Now catching the fish
He never caught

And then:

An independent woman with a great zest for life
Now with her loving husband Jim
This loving couple will now travel through the blue waters

And finally and simply:

Still swimming in the bay

I read the plaques over again and, call it stupid, call it foolish, but I felt my son Cosmo had friends in the water. He wasn't alone.

Tears ran down my face, mixing with the rain.

The sea was up but I was happy. I heard Sarah's laugh and Clem's and Stella's in the wind and the slap of the waves. I was away from home but I had never felt closer to them.

Three Babies: Cosmo

Sarah

I can't remember having an ulterior motive when I declared I was through with birth control. I think I was just that – through with it, not necessarily wanting a baby that minute, or at least not more than anything else. I had always been one to avoid a mortgage and car payments, after all.

I'd always taken on the responsibility – probably due to a fear of pregnancy, AIDS ignorance and an embarrassment to ask for and deal with condoms. I guess by a combination of luck and serial monogamy it had always worked okay. But I was tired of it – tired of the pills and devices, when I didn't mind the idea of a baby and was even getting to the point of liking the idea. So I thought, Let the guy take the responsibility.

The guy at that point was William, my summer fling that had slipped through a year and into another.

I liked William. Well, more than liked, I loved him. I don't know how people can be with someone if they don't think they love them at the time. William made me laugh a lot and was wary enough of me for me to remain in love. If he had obviously fallen for me, I dare say he might have gone the way of a few before him, whom I had invariably left because they liked me too much and therefore had something seriously wrong with their brains. Or, if he hadn't been lovely William, he might have gone the way of the others who were wary and became warier still until they said they needed more time, more space and then were gone.

William did once tell me he needed more space and time to himself. At that point I was living in Melbourne and he was in Sydney and we had no money for plane trips. He seemed to come to Melbourne only when he had an audition. When I pointed out that this wasn't very flattering, he said he would come down one weekend with no other reason than to see me. We would go halves on the fare. On the Thursday, he rang me and started to mumble. I recognised the word 'space'. Realising I was about to be dumped, I interrupted and said he should do the decent thing, be a 'real man' and tell me whatever he had to tell me to my face. While he was collecting his thoughts I hung up.

On the Friday I picked him up at the airport and on the drive to my share house I asked him exactly how much more time and space he needed, given we lived in different cities. He looked sheepish, screwed up his face, avoided eye-contact and mumbled, 'Maybe a bit more?'

I stopped the car, told him to get out and that he could start his 'space and time' immediately. He looked blank. What? I went around to his side and started trying to pull him out. He allowed himself to be pulled out then looked at me pleadingly and made sure I knew I was dumped by adding, 'It's not you, it's me.'

So not just dumped, but dumped permanently. And then, 'Can I still stay at your house tonight? I don't have any money and there's nowhere else for me to go.'

Our memories of that moment differ. I recall shoving him aside to get back into the car as he tripped, staggered and fell. I remember being embarrassed, ashamed, concerned and helping him up.

William says I decked him, my punch knocking all six feet four inches of him off his feet and landing him flat on his back a metre or more away, while I got back into the car and drove off. He says he looked after the retreating car and fell in love.

Either way, he did get back in the car, did come back to my house and somehow he found the time and space.

William wasn't exactly a secure lifestyle catch; his best work at that time was as Santa – a pretty limited season, unfortunately – and he couldn't even get a city gig. In Sydney he was Santa at Liverpool, then when he moved his festive talent to Melbourne, he scored the Frankston Mall, which was okay if he worked for a day, but a two-hour shift actually cost him once he'd paid the train fare. He went anyway. He had his artistic integrity and knew they wouldn't give him work the following full day if he didn't do the two hours.

I wasn't a great catch for him either. I was a newly graduated animator, whose ignorance in quoting had left me earning about twenty cents an hour and working twenty hours a day on the titles for a feature film.

This would have been around the time I gave up birth control.

I think William lasted about three weeks with condoms, then forgot to go to the shop and said, 'Bugger it, let's go without.'

I said, 'Are you sure? *Sure* sure?'

He thought about it for maybe ten seconds and pretty soon we were pregnant. An unemployed actor and a newly graduated animator, no savings, a bomb of a car and the worst landlord in the world.

We were living in a rented house in Footscray, west of Melbourne. Friends had seen a sign in the front yard saying 'To rent'. Cheap. We had grabbed it and been there for about six months. I had always lived in beautiful places. When you're young and moveable, you can find rental properties with friends overlooking beaches, mountains, in the heart of the city. William and I had met when he lived in a share house above the stunning Bronte Beach in Sydney, while I lived on the clifftop at Austinmer, with views north to the national park and south to Wollongong; an incredible beach in front of me and a dramatic escarpment towering behind, both gorgeous for walking and swimming. I could round a corner, unaware, and the breathtaking view would transform my day, the sunshine lifting my mood and the surf curing any hangover. In Footscray it seemed I had to do all that work myself. The only notable thing about our street was that it had the most police call-outs in Melbourne that year; our moods were our own responsibility.

The baby inside me kept growing, the landlord kept stomping into our house without knocking and shouting at us if there was a towel on the floor or the stove wasn't polished. We kept pointing out that it might be good if the back door would actually close, not just for security, but also because in a house with no heating it was getting a little chilly. Our landlord would shout louder.

William went for auditions and I walked most days along Altona Beach, not too far from us. With its flat water and seaweed smell, the signs of hoon-driving along the esplanade and leftover bottles from the night-time parties, it took me a while to grant it its beach status. I walked from the boat club then out along the pier. I'd stop there and watch the water for a while, at first imagining what might lie beneath its opacity – great white sharks, leopard seals – in hope, as much as horror, then becoming mesmerised by the patterns on its surface.

The colours of water are nearly always beautiful to me and I have tried to capture them in my paintings and animations. To animate someone walking, you can keep a satisfying loop going as the same drawings can be re-used as soon as the action is repeated; you draw the person taking one step, then another, then go back to the first drawing again. Water movement in animation also looks like it's on a loop, a perpetual cycle of the same water being moved by wind and tide, the pattern predictable and continuous. But when I try to sketch a similar set of drawings to those used for a human walk, the result never looks right. I have to produce enough drawings of the water to ensure that the eye has forgotten the beginning of the loop before it can start again. Only then do the colours and patterns of reflection dance with perfectly bonded shapes of transparency; the sky, the cliff, the pier or my pregnant self reflecting in a momentary ripple, while little fish, molluscs clinging to pylons and flowing seaweed can be glimpsed in between. The life below the surface is also a cycle – one thing feeding another, empty shells of one creature housing another, the tides flowing in and out – as sure as the sun setting and the moon rising.

Gradually, as the baby inside me grew bigger and bigger, I saw the more subtle beauty the bay beaches offer and, no matter what the weather, I always felt better after my walk, even if I'd felt fine before. The drive home past the oil refinery, a flame perpetually burning, through semi-industrial suburbs, also became familiar, if not exactly beautiful.

We booked into a hospital, where they registered us at a clinic, arranged standard tests and antenatal classes and gave us a due date. We went to the first class, maybe even the first two, together. They talked about babies, birthing, choices and best practice. They told us about things we didn't need, like a change table, though one of the attendees would invariably attempt to persuade the rest of us they were invaluable and where you could buy really nice ones at a twenty per cent discount. They told us what we did need: a car capsule, nappies, clothes, pram, pouches, nipple pads, maternity pads. They showed us videos. Graphic videos.

We left and got in the car to go home. Our car didn't even have seatbelts in the back. How would that work with a capsule? I looked down at my body. How would *that* work? I looked at William.

'Surely we both don't need to go to this stuff?' I said.

He nodded in agreement, unable to hide the look of hope as it stirred in his heart, which I then crushed by pointing out that as I was the one who had to give birth, I shouldn't have to be the one forced to endure the graphic videos. Or the question-and-answer sessions. Or the chats about names with the girls at the urn as we made cuppas for the hubbies who were talking football. I should be the one who stayed home and kept the television company and the cappuccino-swirl ice-cream under control. When the birth came he could just pass on the relevant information as required.

So William went off to the antenatal classes by himself, the only non-couple except for a brave and probably normally sane single mother-to-be, who, in competitive couple-land, was understandably defensive and grumpy. How could I not love the man?

Each week he came home to find me either in floods of tears over the cute puppy on the dog food commercial or the poor children who had been highlighted in the news, or to wake me up by gently taking the empty carton of ice-cream from my hands. He'd tell me the stories of the other people's lives – marble bathroom renovations, family implosions, hilarious weddings.

It's not that easy to avoid information, though. Friends of friends of sisters-in-law give you cots, baby clothes, nappies and books on birthing and babies. They tell you their own birth war stories, feel your belly as if it isn't a part of your body anymore and normal rules don't apply. Strangers in the street quite happily give you a pat or feel for kicks.

I did sneak looks at birthing books that were lent and decided I'd like the birth to be as natural as possible, though within the safety net of the hospital system.

I passed all the tests with flying colours, looked rudely healthy, as usual, and felt fine. All except for one test, that is, which apparently was only done in the midwives' clinic

I had been assigned to as part of a medical trial. They were testing to see if low estriol levels in pregnant women were related to low birth weight and therefore more at-risk babies. I didn't pass and did have low estriol levels.

I agreed to be in the trial. I believe in medical research. Why wouldn't I? I am very glad to be alive in the time of anaesthetics, penicillin and Ventolin. I like the idea of a cure for cancer. I doubted whether a pieceworker and an underemployed actor were going to contribute much to that discovery any other way. And it meant being given vitamins, amino acids. It seemed designed for low socio-economic, junk-food-eating, smoking, alcoholic drug users, and I didn't see what harm they could do me, who was currently none of the above.

All I had to do was spend every second or third weekend in hospital being fed vitamins and amino acids by a drip. It would either make no difference or presumably we would produce a super baby, who could ease William's concern for his football and cricket teams being that one vital player short. It meant being pushed from the midwives' clinic to the doctors' clinic, but I didn't want to argue with that; the birth wasn't as important to me as the baby, and maybe this estriol thing did mean something. I'd given up smoking and drinking to have this baby, so why would I baulk at a couple of weekends?

The first time I went I was nervous – a stranger to hospitals and scared, mostly of being bored. I shared the ward with six others. One woman, Mandy, was in for the same reason as me. A bouncy, gorgeous and obviously healthy girl who wore great pyjamas. Elisa, who was having twins, was there on bed rest and this was her second month in the same corner bed. Her side table piled with medical books, she was virtually doing a medical degree. Some slip of early womb organisation had left one twin getting too much growth and the other not enough. Both were likely to die, one definitely. She wanted to save both. The doctors didn't know how.

The patients in the other three beds came and went; some as new mothers with their tiny scrunched-faced newborns, some to be on bed rest, hoping to prevent a miscarriage. It was a room that witnessed pain, heartache and grief daily, but mostly the anticipation of joy and absolute joy.

Mandy, Elisa and I became friends as Mandy and I did the same weekends and Elisa was always there, her twins clinging on, inching towards viability. Mandy had a Greek Adonis husband – hair down his back, motorcycle helmet under his arm – who would sneak in with chocolate, champagne and a Scrabble board at midnight. Mandy and I, with our long-line drips, would play and try to keep our giggles from waking the others. William would bring me real coffee in the mornings. On the Monday afternoon we'd go home, full of stories and vitamins.

William got a part in a play and I got another animating job and quoted myself up to maybe a dollar an hour. I was to draw ten thousand pictures of endangered animals for a television series, *The Web of Life*.

We had seatbelts fitted in the back seat of the Falcon.

He endeared himself to my non-theatre-going father when, in a pivotal scene, a cast-mate forgot his line, agonised silently, then decided acting was no longer his thing and walked off-stage and out of the theatre. The audience was silent and unsure what was going on. My father, in the front row with my mum, felt as much embarrassment for other people as he did for himself, a trait I unfortunately inherited. It leaves you perpetually embarrassed about something and unable to enjoy slapstick comedy. Dad went red and sank back in his seat as William, waiting for his feed line, stood alone on the stage. Suddenly, William started to sing the Collingwood Football Club song – word perfect – in its entirety. Everyone laughed, my father not only amused and relieved but also very impressed this blow-in from Queensland knew all the words.

During the days I drew the endangered animals, learning more of the tough laws of animal life and how we fit into the biological web yet seem so often to forget we are just animals ourselves. I would often work in my pyjamas until it was warm enough to brave the windswept bathroom, thanks to the uncloseable back door. So it was late one morning that I was getting dressed in front of the two-bar radiator, when the landlord burst in unannounced, shouting for his rent in advance. As I dithered with my bra strap and covered myself with a towel, not sure whether dressing in front of weird horrible men isn't just as bad as undressing in front of them, I pointed out that we had paid him a month's rent in advance just last week.

'I need the money now! Give me the cash!'

'I don't have any cash.'

'You must!' he shouted, and started looking in containers around the house. He was almost psychotic, raving as he invaded. His English was patchy, but I picked up enough to know that I was an unmarried whore and both me and my village idiot would be going to hell and someone would kill William if the landlord didn't get the money today.

It was time to move.

William had received a tax return from his play, it being his only job that year. I sold a painting. He had a small role in a TV series coming up. A 'For sale' sign triggered us into thinking the impossible. Us? Buy a house?

I don't think either of us had ever dreamt we would own a house, but at the time there was a property slump, no one was buying, a home in Footscray could be had for sixty-thousand and they got cheaper the further west you ventured. We ventured to West Footscray.

We went to the bank. This was in the day when the local bank manager was in charge and could approve loans, rather than a centralised impersonal check system. We went to the bank with our new balance and applied for a loan.

We sat waiting, nervously, in our best 'we are responsible debt-paying citizens' clothes, looking at the people of West Footscray trailing in and out; a very diverse mix, but perhaps a little under-represented by the upper echelons of wealth and power.

We were called in to a screened-off section. The manager looked doubtfully at our references, our savings history, our lack of steady employment. It didn't seem promising until he said the magic words: 'Don't I know you from somewhere?'

William admitted he had recently been on an episode of 'A Country Practice'.

'So you're a TV star? So you'll be getting lots of work?'

'Yes, of course,' said William.

Obviously this was not the time to point out that he only had two days on the show, was paid award minimum and had barely sniffed work since.

The bank manager sat back in his chair, thinking. We waited.

He finally spoke. 'TV, eh? You can earn a lot of money on TV.'

We didn't point out that ninety-five per cent of actors are unemployed at any given time, and half of those employed are on contracts where they have to be available every day for weeks yet are only paid when they are called in for the odd day. And theatre acting was like being a painter, a hobby that if it occasionally earned you enough to buy more art materials meant you were a success.

The bank manager thought some more, then he looked up. 'What's that girl who plays Molly really like? She has to be lovely. She's so lovely.' He looked with respect at William, now two degrees only from his TV crush.

We got the loan.

Our renovators' delight was opposite the Tottenham shunting yards, a wide flat expanse of the country, interstate and suburban railway lines and container trains. On the other side were the remnants of industry: the Uncle Toby's silo, Watts wool stores. The sky arched wide over us. It had the feel of a remote country town, yet the city silhouette was at the end of our street. We could have chooks and walk to the city in less than an hour. At night the whole area was lit by hanging strings of lights. It was like fairyland.

We had two bedrooms, an outside toilet brought inside by a lean-to and a good inch of tobacco waste-product covering all surfaces and walls. But the garden was huge and wild, the backyard faced north, it had a shed and the front and back doors not only closed but locked.

We would take possession the week the baby was due. Apparently it's a rule with first babies: make life more difficult for yourself.

On my last weekend drip session there was no Mandy in the bed opposite. She was downstairs giving birth. She came up the next day and showed off the prettiest baby girl with the blackest curls and bluest eyes. Mandy was a mother with her own crying baby complete with little waving arms and legs and perfect fingers and toes. I couldn't believe that would be me any time in the next month. I tried to hold the baby, so awkwardly, her head rolling, feeling as if I would squash or drop her. She cried and Mandy took her back, looking into her face and rocking her so naturally. Could I do it? Me?

The clinic wanted me to be induced if my labour hadn't started by my due date. So on that day we packed up everything on our checklist: pyjamas, baby clothes, nappies, music, William's class notes and our friend Rose. So excited. So nervous. How much exactly was this going to hurt?

A lot. They had broken my waters the night before, but when that had not started the contractions during the long and sleepless night, they hooked me up to some drugs and started them for me. No lead-up, no gentle tugs becoming stronger, this was a frog thrust straight into the boiling water. Wham. Induce? This needed a better word; induce implies more carrot than stick.

'William? What do I do?'

'I don't know. Breathe.'

'I *am* bloody breathing!'

Rose put some music on. I walked around. The second contraction hit. I got on the bed.

A nurse came in to see how we were going and we swapped jokes. She listened to the baby's heartbeat. She listened again. Then tried a new place. She avoided eye contact and left.

William and I looked at each other, then the third contraction hit and I couldn't think until it subsided. A doctor was there, then two, then three. They turned off the drug supply. There was no heartbeat. Our baby was dead.

No rushing to theatre, no drama, no panic. Just quiet.

I was only one centimetre dilated, but the cord had managed to slip down beside the baby's head and the contractions had pushed his head against the cord, squashing it and suffocating him. His head hadn't been engaged when they broke the waters. He just wasn't ready.

There was silence for a while, Rose's tears being the first to come. A nurse wiped her eye.

'Well, I'm afraid we've still got to get this baby out,' one of the doctors said.

I begged for them to put me to sleep, to just cut the baby out of me. But there was no reason for a Caesarean: I wasn't at risk, the baby wasn't at risk.

Sixteen hours of heavy labour to deliver a dead baby.

But then he was born and they laid him on my chest. A boy. A beautiful big baby boy. And I looked at him and felt that same love and amazement that most women have at that time. My beautiful boy was well above average weight. Perfect except for suffocation.

I wanted to hold him for ever. William bathed him. Rose held him. I held him again.

We named him Cosmo Robert Colin McInnes and held him for hours as the warmth of his little body seeped away and the dawn light edged into the room.

They took Cosmo away, eventually persuading me to let him go by promising I could visit him 'downstairs' at any time.

William made some of the hardest phone calls he has ever had to make, and then he went to work. I actually encouraged him. He was so befuddled with shock and didn't know what to do.

'Well, you said you'd go, you should go. Be good. Don't make a fuss. You love your job.' I was obviously brainless as well.

There are many ways of being Herculean. William spent his first child's birthday and death in a Hawaiian shirt, playing a drunk Aussie at a Melbourne Cup Day party in a fictional South-East Asian country. He didn't tell anyone about the reason for his exhaustion and there were many hangover jibes. There was a fight scene and he had to look like he was landing punches. In another scene he had to laugh loudly, feigning genuine amusement. He had to act well enough and be pleasant enough to impress the director and producers so he could get another job one day. He did it all.

They took me from the delivery room to a ward. The same kind of ward I had been in before. Two new mothers with their babies, one sleeping, one crying as he and his mother struggled to make contact for the first feed with the help of a nurse. And two very pregnant women waiting. I felt like a leper.

I visited Cosmo in the cold room, led by a nun through unadorned corridors, past the industrial kitchens, the back-up generators and the loading docks to the hospital morgue in the basement. The failure room. The nun wanted to come in with me. It was the rule.

I said, 'No thanks.'

There was a minor silent stand-off until she relented and sat just outside.

They had brought Cosmo out for me, into a side room. Down the corridor I could glimpse stainless steel, but in this room a small bunch of artificial flowers sat on a table alongside social-work pamphlets and a box of tissues.

Cosmo lay in a crib, wrapped in his baby blue hospital blanket. I looked at him for a long while. He had odd patches of colour, blood pooling instead of pumping, but he didn't look dead to me. This was my baby, our baby, and the only way I knew him.

Almost as if I were doing something naughty, I checked the nun wasn't looking, then picked him up and held him, as gently as Mandy had held her little girl. Then I undressed him. He was perfect. A little chubby, dark hair, wide face, a generous mouth and strong forehead. Like his mother.

I put on the miniature clothes I had bought for him – the cute singlet and soft pants. They were a little small for him. I wrapped him back up in his blanket and held him for hours, until the nun had to ask the doctors to put him back in the big fridge.

A senior doctor came to see me back in the ward. He glanced at my family, who had come to visit, muttered his condolences – 'Pity about that baby' – then left quickly, before we could say anything; the first of many doctors who never said the word that might have started my healing. Sorry.

William came in after work and went off with the obligatory nun to hold Cosmo. He came back and was quiet.

My mother came to see him. I proudly showed off her grandson. She touched his face gently. 'He's so cold.'

'But isn't he beautiful?' I said.

She nodded.

'Do you want to hold him?'

She paused, then slowly shook her head. 'You hold him.'

So I did and she sat with me. The mother, and the daughter trying to mother. There wasn't much to say; we weren't the hugging and crying kind. I wanted to take Cosmo home and keep him in our freezer, seriously. Even William couldn't come at that.

I didn't and he was cremated. We had a service, our friends and family came and shared their love. I held myself together. My arms physically ached with emptiness.

_____

We went back to the hospital. What had happened? They told us that he always had a chance of dying; he was in the clinical trial and five per cent of babies in that study die. We didn't say anything. I knew I was furious and confused, but unfortunately I was a politeness hostage. It was like saying that it didn't really matter that he was hit by a bus because he had a small freckle that one day could become cancerous. No. It was like saying, 'It doesn't matter that he was hit by the drunk driver, because he lived in Melbourne.' To this day I think of replies at 3 a.m. And I still want to say to them, 'There was nothing wrong with him. Why don't you just say sorry, you stuffed up?'

With the help of good friends we moved into our new house. An awful day of bad jokes and long silences, taking load after load in our car and a borrowed ute. All that lent baby stuff, trip after trip of now useless things and meaningless art materials and possessions. Into our new meaningless house.

The little box of Cosmo's ashes I took on my lap, still reluctant to allow even William into my loss, never mind acknowledge his or anyone else's.

We grieved in the way people do, at different times with clashing needs and stages. I don't know why William stuck with me, but I stuck with him because I knew his loss and his learning were as great as mine.

People were good or not. Small or big tragedies, some people will cross the road to avoid you while others will cross the road to give you enough kindness and generosity to call the world even.

One day I went to the shops – strange that you still eat, still work, still go through the motions – and came back with a puppy. Someone was giving him away, the runt of a litter of farm kelpie crosses. It took me about three seconds to decide. We called him Doug. The black Douglas. Doug Hawkins. Doug was more joey than puppy, barely allowed on the ground with either Will or I wanting to hold him.

We scattered Cosmo's ashes from the pier. Some floated, some fell to the bottom to join the other small treasures there. Some of him to float away, to anywhere the tides and winds carried him, some to be glimpsed between the reflections of the sky on the water.

Three Babies: Clem

Sarah

Our second baby was born, and he breathed. Then he cried. I sobbed. I guess with joy – it was hard to tell because I was so embarrassed. And as I write I am ashamed to confess that I actually got embarrassed at such a time, when emotions should be free and real and embraced. But there were a lot of people in the room, and as the one with the big belly, the Caesar cut and the baby, it was pretty hard to avoid centre stage.

My first gift to our second son – the potential to be embarrassed, to deny yourself a good joyful weep, because you're too self-conscious. Years later it would take me weeks to coax him out of the car to sign up for the cricket club he desperately wanted to join or into the water he loved because he thought his bathers weren't right. His was a tiny newborn cry, all his own. I smiled at everyone as politely as I could through the tears. Thank you, thank you, thank you.

We had gone back to the same hospital, been closely monitored and sad enough to make the staff treat us with kid gloves. I had a Caesarean. For a while I had thought of going somewhere else to give birth, an African field perhaps or a warm bath at home, but I knew I wouldn't cope, wondering where that slippery umbilical cord was during the labour. So we decided I would have a Caesar in the same hospital, the same public system.

William carefully took the baby from the delivering doctor and held him as if he were the most fragile of bubbles. They looked at each other and then, though I'm sure

William never wanted to let him go, he gave him to me to hold. Swallowing my sobs into laughter, I held him; another beautiful boy. I checked him over – a long body, brilliant blue eyes, a perfectly rounded, unsquished head. A mini William. William and I held hands and looked proudly at what we had made. We named him Clement Vaughan Galloway McInnes, after the grandfathers and William's brother.

He was as full of vitamins as Cosmo had been. I had again been tested halfway and again had low estriol levels, the only not-completely-normal aspect of the pregnancy. I had again spent my weekends in hospital being pumped with amino acids and vitamins, pumped full of knowledge about the amazing things some people go through.

William took Clem away with a nurse, I thought at the time to bathe him, hold him and dress him, while I was stitched up and moved to the ward. In hindsight I can see that of course William used this time to bond with Clem and pass on to him the secret world of McInnes, a complicated world of funny voices, excellent imitations, shower singing, various sets of strict moral codes from which sport is invariably excused and, of course, hyperactivity of an oddly indolent kind.

In the ward I lay in a bed next to a woman who had also just given birth and was holding her newborn in a pink blanket. We exchanged smiles and grimaces. Her husband came in from work, having missed the birth. He kissed his wife dutifully, looked at the baby and tried not to sigh, failing. The woman seemed embarrassed and explained to me that he had wanted a boy. I must have looked horrified, so she tried to defend him.

'We really thought this would be a boy. The last four were supposed to be boys. It's the seventh girl.'

The man shook his head sadly, and repeated, 'No boys yet. And you?'

I smiled apologetically. 'A boy.'

The man smiled again.

The woman said, 'Your husband will be happy.'

'I think he would have loved a girl,' I said.

The woman shrugged. 'They say that. Your first?'

I hesitated, then made the first of many small betrayals to my Cosmo and nodded. Easier.

By the time William brought Clem back I was almost embarrassed to have such good fortune. The next-bed husband came over to see him. Clem burped. The husband turned to his wife.

'Look, he burped!'

She nodded. 'That's nice.'

Clem yawned.

'Look, he's yawning!' He laughed with delight. 'I've never seen our girls yawn so early.'

She nodded again, tiredly.

'Look how long he is, how big his feet are. He's going to be a big strong boy, aren't you, little boy?'

He was now bent over Clem in such adoration I nearly said we'd swap if it would make everyone happier. William, perhaps guessing that I would go that far just to get out of the conversation, went over to admire the new baby girl in such glowing terms that the father drifted back to his wife. And the six other beautiful little girls who eventually visited.

Clem was still in his hospital wrap and blanket. We had no clothes for him, no nappies. I hadn't wanted to jinx the birth by being prepared in any way. Though we had stayed in our new house I had given everything baby-like onwards. There was no cot, no pram, no capsule in the car waiting. No clothes, no toys.

William went shopping and I tried to breastfeed. Breastfeeding. What can I say? Worse than giving birth, as far as I was concerned. We tried for a while, Clem and I, and maybe he got a bit of milk into him, but we were soon so frazzled with our efforts that we were both crying; him loudly and freely, me embarrassed, full of self-pity.

As soon as I could get up I walked him tentatively up and down the wide glassed-in verandah. The windows all along one side looked out over beautiful gardens, a speciality of Melbourne. At the end of the corridor you could look over into a football field, another speciality of Melbourne. It was September, footy finals season. There was a game on and we could hear that weird beckoning sound of a crowd shouting in unison. Clem gradually stopped crying. He seemed soothed by the noise. Or perhaps he had a glimpse of the football when a long drop punt rose high enough. I was unknowingly consolidating William's early work.

I battled on with the breastfeeding – bleeding nipples, cabbage leaves, mastitis and many tears in the shower. Thank God it was pre-drought. I couldn't believe there were still worse aspects to being female. Isn't getting your period at twelve enough? Isn't that the moment we learn to shove pain and moods under the carpet as best we can? But now this, the highest form of multi-tasking: being hugely in love and loving to a small creature you have so desired, so needed and are so thankful for that he makes all else in the world seem less important, if important at all, while at the same time allowing this very baby to inflict a minor form of torture on your body. Eventually, we got the hang of it and it was great, easy and lovely, but it took a while.

William was wonderful, always walking him up and down. Singing to him. Al Martino seemed to work quite well. I am glad, though, for Clem, that William hadn't discovered Val Doonican at that stage.

But it seemed I couldn't do anything right. Clem needed me every second, needed my body, my total attention and yet still was not satisfied, still he cried. Evil thoughts crept into my head. Cosmo hadn't been hard. Cosmo didn't cry all night. Cosmo was perfect. Cosmo looked like me. Clem was all William.

I didn't share this information with anyone. I tried not to think it. I didn't even believe it myself. I have many photos of Clem, as many as an addicted photographer and besotted new mother can take. In many of them he is smiling and gurgling, in others he is angelically calm and content. Presumably, life wasn't that bad all the time. Sometimes I would sit quietly with him in the night, feeding him. We would look at each other while he sucked, as one. One night he gradually slowed then stopped sucking. We still stared at each other. Seemingly for an hour. Just looking, perhaps searching each other's souls, perhaps simply both too tired to do anything else. I felt I was holding someone good, someone who would do good in the world. And, slowly, something was thawing in me. There was no sudden realisation, no epiphany, gradually Clem just became Clem to me; not a baby who was crying, but my Clem, who wanted something or was hurt. Clem, who made me smile. Clem of the good heart, never to be mistaken for anyone but himself. Clem, whom I love.

As I fumbled my way into being a mother, I was becoming a filmmaker at the same time. I had received the go-ahead to make a short animated film I had written while pregnant. In the way of the world of babies, the first cheque and therefore deadline had come in the mail the day before we had Clem.

Our house gradually filled with baby things, as well as art materials and audition notes and scripts. Crying became rare and laughing common. Clem soon crawled, said his first words and laughed along with us. He slept with a football. He preferred it to his teddy. 'Boys will be boys,' people would say. I think William put a little honey on it to get him started.

When Clem was born, the 'bloke' in William ascended; he called Clem 'mate', and sport was heaven. It suited me in a way. If William was at one of his hopeful auditions or doubly nervous call-backs or stopping by the pub on the way home from a rejection, I had not only 'Thomas the Tank Engine' to entertain Clem, but any number of sporting codes.

I often do some of the rote work of animation in front of the television. Like my mother before me, it always seemed wrong to just sit; you had to sit and knit or shell peas or clean your school shoes. I don't believe any of these activities have ever occurred in our house, but I did do my colouring-in. Animation is about two per cent creativity and brain work and the rest is rote. That's why I like it. Those art forms that require the stats to be the other way round are just too stressful and do nothing for a person who has inherited both Catholic guilt and the Protestant work ethic in spades.

I don't love watching sport on TV, apart from the Olympics, which unfortunately aren't televised on a daily basis throughout the year, though that is probably why I watch them. Clem couldn't seem to get excited about murder mysteries. He liked weather documentaries, but when he began to get paranoid about the big twisty winds in the middle of the night, I thought it best to ease up a little. We finally found a middle ground in fishing shows. We'd watch a couple of men catching fish in all sorts of beautiful places. They'd either kiss their catches and pop them back in the water, where they swam away happily or make them the centrepiece at a barbecue.

One day, when Clem and I were barramundi fishing in the Northern Territory, the occasional crocodile shot keeping my pencil mid-air and Clem clinging to my neck in raptures, the phone rang and our lives changed somewhat. William had been offered a big job.

He'd won a part in a TV show called 'Blue Heelers'. He went from uncertainty about whether he would ever get a job to uncertainty that it was the right job, to uncertainty that this would be the only acting job he would ever get. I didn't know then that this process was the norm, but have since learnt it's unavoidable.

We worked through it. It was money, he would be practising his craft and he could support his family. But a television cop show wasn't the normal route taken to become the new Alec Guinness or a famed Shakespearean master. What if it failed and he never got another job? What if it succeeded and he never got another job? What *did* happen to those people on 'A Country Practice'? We could name one or two still working, but what about the others? Did Molly ever get another job? Would she ever be anyone but Molly in Australian eyes?

William eventually decided that it didn't sound too bad, had a good cast, and that if he got out before Mount Thomas was invaded by giant ants or he was abducted by an alien, he might still have a career. Or maybe the mining industry would have opened up a little.

The series was a hit and though William did his best to avoid ever being on the cover of *TV Week*, he began to be recognised. Never as William McInnes and not always as Nick Schultz from 'Blue Heelers', but as 'someone'. An ex-footballer? Rugby? AFL? Cricket? Occasionally the nasty cop who put someone's relation in jail or gave them a speeding ticket. Lois, one of our louder local eccentrics, took a long time to stop swearing at him for being 'A bloody screw!', an impression that was harder to shake because once she saw William get on the local bus at the remand centre. Now she just shouts at him for no reason, like she shouts at everyone else.

Having a recognisable husband is fertile ground for someone who suffers from self-consciousness. I had times when I nearly died as people who thought they knew him continued to dig themselves deeper.

'You were stationed with my brother. It must have been at Tarneit.'

William would begin to shake his head.

'Or when he was up in the Mallee. It was you. Remember you came to our house once and you and George locked the pig in the bathroom?'

By this stage my nails would be bleeding as I bit them, knowing how bad the speaker would feel when the truth was revealed. Sometimes it never was, William having as good a laugh as the strangers over the time with the pig, even convincing me he had actually been there. Sometimes when they found out they were even more pleased, no embarrassment at all on their part.

It is a bit hard to say when people get it wrong, 'No, you know me from the TV.' It sounds so smug and arrogant. Hard for William. Virtually impossible for me. And it was often me.

People would come up to me, confessing that they were unwilling to interrupt William or embarrass him, but was he 'the guy off "Blue Heelers"?' I didn't mind that so much, when they got it right; I would just nod and slink away, while they looked back in awe at having seen someone from the television. Which I always am, too. That's why it's all so embarrassing; I am one of them.

Clem and I saw a familiar newsreader in the supermarket once and smiled and said hello. The poor man gave a non-eye-contact minimal smile, abandoned the cereal he was buying and scurried away, doubtless worried I was about to start asking how the kids were or something. I then realised who he was, so familiar to me, while I was just another mad woman to him. I was still so excited. It was the highlight of our day and we eagerly reported it to William when he got home that night.

There are long working days in the television industry. In most areas of film and television productions, leaving work at 5 p.m. is like going home before lunch. The actors often have to be there early for make-up and long cosy chats over coffee or manic learning of lines, while the crew work hard to set up the different shots of the day. And they need a lot of shots, shooting an hour-long episode over four days, the fifth being for rehearsal. It's hardly like being down in the mines, or in the production line at Ford, but the hours are pretty long.

So Clem and I were thrown together more. I would get through the day okay, keeping Clem alive, getting just enough of my work done during his sleeps and periods of self-entertainment.

Rip up the newspaper while Mum does twenty drawings, take everything out of the drawers for another ten, eat all those hundreds and thousands one by one and Mum will be right with you!

At about 6 p.m., that special time of day when the child is overactive and overtired and the mother is just over it, I would pour myself a glass of wine and wait for the call from whomever William would have persuaded – or bribed – into calling me to tell me that he'd be late. Then Clem and I would watch a fishing show.

We began to actually *go* fishing, driving down to the pier. I would look at the water and say a silent hello to Cosmo. At first we watched other people fish, looked through the gaps between the wooden slats of the pier into the water below, and threw our ice-cream cones to the seagulls. Then one day Clem saw an old man catch a fish, and suddenly watching wasn't enough any more.

At home I dug out my rod and some hand reels buried beneath other assorted litter from my life and handed the rod to Clem. As well as high excitement, I saw a new respect for me in his eyes; maybe just a suspicion that I might eventually provide recreation as well as food, baths and boundaries.

We went back to the pier. Even at this young age Clem, with undoubtedly inherited instincts, was aware that the rest of the world obviously knew what to do in any given activity, while we didn't. So we found a place away from anyone who may have been helpful, thus forever compounding our amateur status.

Fish are really hard to catch. Those people on TV have the advantage of knowledge, a budget and, most importantly, editing. We had none of these, but did have the added problem of Clem being unable to sit still for five minutes. But we tried. We caught seaweed fish and the odd litter fish. We lost hooks on giant sharks, weird deep-sea fish with their own lights that were in one of Clem's books, barramundi like the guy on TV and sometimes rocks. Which was fine with me. I wasn't sure I wanted either of us to actually catch anything.

I remember being about thirteen and on a family holiday on the south coast, when I caught the fishing bug. Everyone else spent their time at the rollerskating rink or the beach, but I sat doggedly and daggily on a pier day after day with a bucket, hand-line and sinker and bits of sandwich meat on a single hook.

Mostly I had bites, sudden jerks on the line that I'd quickly wind in, only to find a bare hook, no bait and no fish. Sometimes I did get lucky. The jerks on the line would continue and I'd pull the creature up, enjoying the little tussle until I'd delightedly lift the fish onto the pier, gorgeous flashing silver in the sunshine as it leapt about on the hook. I'd be ecstatic. For a moment.

Then I'd look at it, this tiny thing, so real and alive, a great big hook wedged in its throat, sometimes through its gills. I'd try to pick it up, too hesitantly, often dropping it to flop about on the pier, the poor little thing panicking, unable to breathe. I'd finally find a grasp on it and try to remove the hook, guilt and panic almost overwhelming me as its struggles became weaker and weaker.

Sometimes, the hook would come out and I'd quickly drop the fish back into the water. It would lie there, motionless, just below the surface. I'd look around guiltily, hoping, praying that no one was witnessing this low point of my life. This ineptitude, this murder. Then the fish would suddenly revive and swim quickly away into the deep and relief and happiness would wash over me.

I'd bait up and do it again, because next time I'd be catching a big fish, a real fish to take home for dinner, for everyone to be proud of me around the barbecue. And then, of course, I'd catch another baby fish.

Later, in my twenties, I took up fishing again with my friend Rose. I met her at a bar when we simultaneously ordered a strawberry daiquiri, both of us looking for sunshine on a rainy night. We caught a few real fish. And ate them. I bought my own rod and gear. I loved being in little boats and on piers or hanging over a bridge.

Once, we went surf-fishing on a beautiful wild and windy beach, standing knee-deep in the water to be lapped by the waves, coated with salt and negative ions.

I thought I had caught yet another rock fish and was going to lose my hook and sinker again, but I managed to wind the line in a little. It felt like a huge weight, coming and going with the surf surges. Maybe a moving rock or a giant kelp fish, it was almost impossible to drag in. Then, as I wound in more line, the weight started to feel more fish-like. I had to let the line out for it, then furiously take it up when it slackened. I began to feel like a hunter, excited. I was in the grip. I saw a flip of silver as the fish leapt out of the water in its struggles. I began to feel it through the line, feel when I needed to let line out, when to pull hard, when to pull softly; a master hunter. Eventually, I pulled in a medium-sized mullet, got the hook off by myself, cleaned and filleted the fish and later we made an excellent curry.

And now here I was, back on a pier, with a son – my big, gorgeous, still-my-baby son. What to do? Which part of me to pass on? The master hunter of the seas or the bleeding heart on the pier? Was it even up to me? Are children their true selves already or are you holding in your hand the future of the world and your small part in shaping it? Do you tell them that the scar on your head was from falling down drunk and hitting the coffee table on your way (William) or from not wearing your seatbelt as a teenager (me)? Will they take that as a lesson and learn or as an instruction pamphlet to follow unthinkingly?

I didn't want Clem to be a heartless person. But we ate fish, and I wanted him to eat fish, not just the chips. It's good to see the reality of life, surely? Or was I just indulging him because of a television show and all those happy smiling men with their great big fish, hoping he would be more confident in himself? How do you walk the fine line of making them fit in just enough without indulging their every whim? My eighty-year-old mother still talks about the horror of being sent to school in the wrong length socks when she already had to wear glasses and was a year older than the other kids. She was demonstrably scarred for life, yet still hand-knitted our school jumpers; in hindsight, of course, this was an act of love as well as thrift, not the social punishment I thought it at the time. Also in hindsight I realised I would have been self-conscious about anything; a dress a centimetre too long or too short, the wrong-coloured pencils, a freckle.

We kept fishing on the pier, Clem and I. We caught a few rock and seaweed fish and perhaps that would have been the end of it if Clem hadn't had a bite. A big jerk on the line. No bait on the hook when it was pulled in. His excitement was joyful. What had

it been? A massive snapper, a passing tuna, maybe even a great white shark? We had fun and Clem was hooked.

William kept up his work in shaping Clem, taking him to football matches, explaining to him at length the rules, which teams were evil, which were bearable, which you could barrack weakly for if your team missed out on the finals, why this particular player was to be reviled and this one adored, why the umpires are usually wrong, what he should do in any given situation of play. That sort of stuff.

Cricket season was heaven for both of them, imitating the commentators a favourite sport. Clem had Richie Benaud down pat at three and Tony Greig not long after. They would do their own commentary. They had lunch breaks and would go out on the street to hit a few balls. Or kick a few balls.

But Clem never lost the passion for fishing, though William didn't really mention it, never mind encouraging it. We went a few times, the 'three of us', which only served to keep Clem wanting more. Inevitably, he caught his first fish and the joy was worth it. I took a photo then removed the creature from the hook, remembering just enough, getting it off in time for Clem to kiss it and gently throw it back. We survived the agony of the motionless float, then cheered and clapped when it swam away.

The three of us again went fishing together in Redcliffe, where we always holiday, often against all reason. Redcliffe Peninsula has a great pier – well, actually an unused bridge, running alongside the new bridge, which now runs alongside the *new* new bridge. It is three kilometres long with a couple of bumps for the boats to go under, so there is plenty of room to walk along and find a lonely spot to set up your chairs, thermos and bait without embarrassing the people who know what to do.

Looking west over the water to the uninhabited mangroves, wetlands and mountains is beautiful at any time of the day. But at dusk, at fishing time, it is stunning. Birds fly in from their day, trailing long shadows then kicking up pink and orange sparkles as they skim the water to land. The sky is huge and brilliantly coloured. The light is breathtaking, and apparently people actually catch fish.

We fished a little in our unsuccessful way, then I went for a walk. I like to look at birds, a hobby inspired in me by my mother, an avid birdwatcher. I use a camera instead of binoculars, which, due to the vagaries of light and movement, makes identifying the bird harder. But birdwatching is like fishing, it takes you to places, often magical places, where you can just stand or wander around for hours with a purpose. And capturing a bird with a camera is a lot less messy than fishing.

I was walking back towards William and Clem when I saw Clem reeling something in. I paused, hoping he had caught a real fish, an edible fish, but not really wanting to have to deal with any fish, never mind a baby one.

Clem pulled the wriggling thing up onto the pier. A fish! From this distance it didn't seem that small. I could see Clem bravely start to try to get it off the hook. He struggled and William stepped in to help with the eagerness of a meticulous person, nails freshly painted, forced to pluck a maggot-infested feral pigeon.

It is funny yet agonising to watch my husband and son attempt to do something together. There is much shouting, much laughing at the other's pain and wailing at one's own. It is loud and the movements are large. There is slapstick randomness that a Three Stooges routine would find hard to match, usually compounded by taking out pain and frustration not only on each other but on inanimate objects. There is yelping.

Over the years, I've witnessed them attempt to put up a tent, do the dishes, strap a kayak on the car and put together anything involving written instructions, but moving a couch through two doorways and down a hallway is my all-time favourite. High point or low point, I'm not sure.

I walked closer to Clem and William on the pier, unable to help myself. Clem had caught a toadfish, an ugly toxic thing covered in prickles.

I arrived as William was shouting, 'Just cut the line! Cut the line!'

Clem wouldn't, trying to grasp the creature with his sandwich to avoid the prickles, so he could free it. He knelt down on the pier to take the weight of the fish off itself. He looked inside its mouth, tried this way then that. He made a disaster of it, but didn't give up until most of its insides were out and its little heart lay beating gently on the pier. Then he cried. In public and witnessed by the people who know what to do.

He was inconsolable.

'I killed it!'

'Darling, they're a feral pest,' I said, most likely completely wrong.

'But I killed it!' he sobbed. 'I could have saved it. I killed it. Its little heart, it was beating. It was *outside* his body!'

I tried to divert him with my standard lecture on why we shouldn't assume everything is male just because all cartoon characters are – unless, of course, they have big breasts or bows and fake eyelashes.

'The heart could be beating outside *her* body,' I said.

Unsurprisingly, Clem's sobs didn't abate. Fishing was over for the day.

William and I hugged him, though it didn't help. He was on his own with his remorse. A little person now, a bloke who isn't really a bloke, a shy person who plays class clown, a person who has to turn a map upside down (William) and won't use the phone (me), a part of both of us with both our weaknesses and strengths. And some bits that must be throwbacks to more distant ancestry; I can't imagine where he got his inability to clean his room, that great big lovely baby of ours.

Away from Home, Again

William

The water was warm, and it got in the way of being quiet. It squelched in between the green and black of the grass. The green was the new shoots and the black was what was left from the burn-off the previous month. It pooled a couple of inches deep around our feet with every step we took and our feet would make a farting sound as we lifted them up and plonked them down again. It got in the way of being quiet. That's what we were trying to be. We were Sarah, Sarah's mum, Anna, and me. And a magpie that for some reason known only to itself had decided to join our party. We were birdwatching and we were on holiday.

Anna has watched and noted birds for as long as I have known her, filling books with sightings and records of the types of birds she has seen. Sarah records with her cameras and stood there now, shooting away at a wader that drifted in and out of a swampy pool, which glistened in the afternoon sun. As for the magpie, he hopped along, tilting his head one way and then another with every step I took. I looked down at the bird, he looked up at me. He appeared quite smart in his black-and-white suit, as if he were off to a do somewhere.

Sarah took a few steps and I noticed that her feet didn't fart as much as mine. I put that down to mine being bigger – and clumsier and generally nosier, if it's possible to have noisy feet. As for the magpie, he hopped along, following closely, and with every fart would dart his head in appreciation of my footwork. In fact, my feet were so noisy that even Anna heard them occasionally. After one spectacular foot-fart and resultant moan when my thong remained stuck in the muck, she turned to me, made a mock horrified face and said, 'Shush, Will!'

I pointed, suddenly, which made her try to follow the direction of my arm. The problem was that I was pointing while trying to pick up my thong and regain my balance from my enthusiastic viewpoint – because I'd pointed at another bird I'd seen, a different type of wader that peeped out from behind a branch and then ducked back into the water.

Anna looked at me and I pointed again, this time with a bit more balance, but in doing so, placed my foot upon my thong with a fart and said, loudly and clearly, 'There!'

The magpie looked up and along my arm, then back at me as if I were an idiot.

Then Sarah turned and asked, 'What?'

'Bird,' I replied.

'Where?' said Anna.

'There!' I said.

'Where?' said Sarah.

'There! There!' And after a pause and another point I finished with an emphatic, *'There!'*

I sounded demented and I put this down to me being new to the intricacies of birdwatching rather than to me being a middle-aged man with an irrational temper and lack of communication skills. It was about the thirty-third time I had done it that morning.

Anna sighed. 'Oh, Will. Where is he pointing, Sarah?'

Sarah looked at me. 'You can yell all you want, but you saying "There!" doesn't tell us where it is.'

I pointed again.

Sarah half-laughed. 'Describe where it is.'

'There! To the right of that tree.'

There were a hundred trees in front of us that all had something to the right of them. I took a deep breath, stepped again and made two foot-farts, the noise of which flushed the bird in fright from where it hid.

'Got him! A so-and-so bird type.'

The camera whirred away and Sarah turned. 'There!' She smiled and shook her head. 'Hopeless,' she said to her mother.

'That bird had a nice call,' I said to Sarah.

She nodded and smiled and foot-farted herself. She made a face as Anna looked towards her then took out a small notebook and wrote down what I had said about the bird's call.

Anna read it and then sighed a little. 'Well, I wouldn't know now.' She shrugged her shoulders and smiled. 'Been quite a while since I've heard anything like that, but it is supposed to be a nice song.'

She had been birding for years but had slowly been losing her hearing. Not being able to hear the song of a bird, of that bird in particular, struck me as very unfair. But life can be like that; the wonderful thing about Anna was that she was happy. Happy to be wading around the back of Redcliffe Aerodrome – yes, it's still called an aerodrome – in wetlands that made you feel you weren't in the back blocks of suburbia but miles from anywhere.

The magpie, having finally had enough, flew up over the swamp and into a tree as a yellow biplane chugged behind it, towards the landing strip. The sky was incredibly blue, and it seemed to me, as the magpie warbled away from the tree branch where it now sat, that it would be hard to find anything as beautiful. Then I foot-farted again. Perhaps holidays are always like that, consecutive days of a heightened awareness of life. Maybe it's not until we slow down that we see a little more of the world, conscious of the things that usually go by unnoticed. On holidays, we go somewhere to be taken outside ourselves a little. And sometimes we go some place completely different.

My gaze drifted back to the friendly yellow plane, making its way across the blue sky, reminding me of the big jets that fly across the Pacific. Clem and I found that it's only when locked in the battery-hen confines of an aeroplane's economy class that we truly appreciate the glorious ruthlessness of economic modelling. What brain came up with the most economically rewarding space between the seats, for instance? I would like to meet that person. I think that person would be descended from a long line of battery-chook farm owners or perhaps various proponents of crimes against humanity. I am certain that person would never fly economy long-haul. This is where we found ourselves on our way to the States, locked behind a man who decided that his seat should be reclined as far back as it could go and just as soon as it could be done on the flight. I felt like Gilligan would have felt if the Skipper had taken the top hammock on 'Gilligan's Island'. Sarah is a magnet for people like this; even on short-haul trips she has the happy knack of sitting behind various bulging Skippers, eager to lay back. But Sarah wasn't on this trip, it was just Clem and me, so I had to deal with the recliner.

The safety demonstration video hadn't even finished when the Skipper crashed back into my stomach, where he stayed for my entire journey across the Pacific. He liked to recline; in fact he was *the* great recliner.

The demonstration video. Now there is a piece of work with a sense of humour.

'Subtly, all planes are different!'

Yes they are, especially the mock plane on the video.

A twelve-year-old Clem stared at the screen and then turned to me. 'Why do they have so much room, Dad, those people on that plane?' His young brain exhibiting the first traces of cynicism towards marketing.

The demonstrating models were doing aerobic exercises in unimaginable comfort and space. It looked like an old Jane Fonda exercise tape when compared with the space actually provided by the plane's seats. The brace position was a happy little idea in case of emergency, but the Great Recliner in front ruled out any realistic attempt at approaching the pose adopted by the cheerful model in the roomy space of the video plane.

The Great Recliner in front of me; I was so close to his head that I could rest my chin on his scalp. Who needs in-flight entertainment when I could content myself with counting his hair follicles? I forced my eyes away from this sight and scanned the cabin for empty seats.

Clem smiled at me and said, 'No joy.'

Instead, I saw the choice of reading favoured by my fellow passengers: bulky books by people with names like Wilbur and Clive and Dan and Eric; books with stories about terrorism and nuclear bombs in suitcases and planes plunging into remote jungles and psychotic killers and conspiracies and a total disregard for human life. I looked at a woman reading such a book by a man called Clive. She smiled at me. 'Just a bit of light reading to pass the time.'

Holiday reading. The world was going mad.

I smiled back.

The in-flight entertainment was good. A small video screen rested in the back of every seat on the plane, shining a bluish glow onto our faces. A channel selection let us see an animated version of the trip we were embarking upon, a clunky plane eking its way across the ocean.

Somewhere over the South Pacific I remembered the voice from the in-flight video and his bland tones informing us to remember to exercise our legs during the flight, so a fair while into the journey I heaved my way out from beneath the recliner in front and took a walk around the aircraft. As I staggered past the seats it was like taking some ghostly trip through the evolution of the human species. Lit by the eerie glow of the seat-back television screens I saw about four hundred of my fellow human beings at their most vulnerable. It was somewhat humbling to pass rows and rows of open-mouthed, spread-eagled people fast asleep. Some seemed to manage better than others. Some, unbelievably, even seemed to be content. Some had necks surrounded by 'peanuts', the cushion that clings to the traveller's neck. I knew this because of the elderly man with a foghorn voice who sat across the way from me. He bellowed to his wife: 'I have to have a peanut. Did you bring my peanut?'

I stared at him and he looked at me with his watery eyes.

'You gotta have a peanut … Yes, sir, you gotta have a peanut.'

He waved a flaccid little bag at me and then he blew into it, sometimes making a noise like a whoopee cushion. When he was done he held it out to me and popped it behind his neck. 'There. My peanut … You gotta have a peanut.'

He then slept soundly with his mouth wide open.

As I looked around the cabin I thought how all the people asleep, peanuts or not, looked like they had been painted by Edvard Munch. An aircraft full of *The Scream*, save for two elderly men: a pair of old Aussie Rules football legends, who were playing each other at checkers, their giant dislocated hands dancing on the controls of their video screens and their grandpa glasses balancing on their noses. Their rumbling laughter wafted up the aisles as they countered each other's moves, only instead of streaking down the members' wing at the MCG they were shoulder to shoulder in economy, high above the waves.

I returned to my seat and thought of telling Clem about them, but that would mean having to wake him up. I looked at him and was reminded how happy his birth made me. How I held him for hours after the midwife gave him to me, just me and him in a little room outside the delivery suite. A few minutes turning into an hour and more. His hand curled up and stretched out like a starfish in front of me and I gave him my finger. His fingers closed around it and I felt the warmth and softness of his skin. He had the tiniest hands.

We were now south of Honolulu, a name that conjures up a raft of romantic images. The Great Recliner had leant back so far that I could see through the gap between the two seats to a computer screen, a laptop, a woman writing.

I have never written a letter like this before. But I must in answer to your note.

When you said you loved me I was speechless … but heartbroken …

I looked away. The Great Recliner heaved. I yelped. Clem stirred a little but it was the man with the peanut who got a fright, woke up and muttered something about hardware shops in Portland.

When I was settled and all was Munch-like again on the plane, I sneaked a look back at the screen. The laptop had been folded away and we, all of us in that clunky plane on the animated screen, were flying high above the sea. I closed my eyes and thought of the broken hearts and friendly footy legends and Edvard Munch and peanuts and felt Clem's hand in mine as I fell asleep.

There are many books and indeed many people who will tell you what recovery procedure you should follow after a long-haul flight. We've come up with a couple.

Sarah likes to walk; as soon as she lands she is away. All those stiff muscles from hours cooped in the battery-hen luxury of economy need to be treated somehow.

Marching through Heathrow we didn't stop. 'This gets the blood going!' she told me.

On the tube and out at Notting Hill and to the hotel, bags dumped and we were off; Sarah Watt's walking tour of the old dart's biggest town. Through Kensington Gardens, we stopped for a few moments at Kensington Palace; it was the tenth anniversary of Princess Diana's death and the palace fences were festooned with floral tributes.

It didn't seem that long ago as we wandered past, ten years. I was at home alone when the first reports came through about her accident in the Paris tunnel. I was supposed to be writing a script for a television show, so any excuse to be drawn away from that was welcome.

It was a Sunday in Australia and the first reports were that she was injured and that Dodi Al Fayed was dead.

'The women's magazines are going to eat this up,' said the announcer and then a short time later the same reporter spoke in a more subdued tone of unconfirmed reports of the death of Diana, Princess of Wales.

I went inside and switched the television on and was greeted by the live BBC coverage. A grim-looking TV anchor confirmed the unconfirmed reports. He looked shaken but also very aware that this was a big moment, a big 'I was the man who announced the death of Diana' important moment.

I watched, not thinking anything really, except how fragile and brief a life can be, and then – almost immediately – what a circus all this was sure to become.

We'll never hear the end of this, I thought. Then the English newsman disappeared and was replaced by a rather rough-looking Australian. He had a habit of nodding his head to one side as he spoke and I recognised him as a sports presenter.

He talked about the event in the way of a sports reporter; I assumed he was the only presenter in the studio and so had been handed the gig.

'Unbelievable news, absolutely tragic, that news of Lady Diana that we've just heard, sadly being snatched away. Tragic and unfortunate news, but life, like the football, goes on. Now, Phil, who do you fancy today in this clash between Frankston and the Northern Bull Ants?'

A co-commentator joined him, uttered a few words of condolence and then got on with dissecting 'this mouth-watering clash'.

I stared and then laughed like a drain.

I laughed again as we walked past the tributes on the fence in London. Sarah looked at me and so I told her the story.

She half-smiled and then said, 'It was sad. Those poor boys.'

I humphed a bit and then started to read some of the tributes.

Queen of Hearts, Diana, we will never forget you, the people's princess.

There was one Hobbytex portrait of the late princess that looked more like the boxer Joe Bugner. Underneath was some doggerel poetry. My eyes flicked across the fences, the dead flowers, the ribbons.

Once, when Sarah and I had been in New York on another of Watt's walking tours, we had marched through the streets and then through Central Park, where we caught snowflakes. We ended up downtown and staggered past the tributes to the victims of the September 11 twin towers collapse. I was slightly surprised how deeply the small pieces of ribbon, material and faded photographs of those whose lives were lost affected us both.

We walked away without saying much and found ourselves in Battery Park, shrouded by shadows of the giant statues of remembrance to wartime dead and merchant mariners lost at sea.

Left to the perils of the sea, the survivors later perished.

We had a stand-up row – over what, I can't remember. It doesn't really matter, because soon we were silent and then both in tears and slumped into each other's arms as the Staten Island ferry continued on its course.

Away from home, you watch more, see more, feel more.

It was there – in the shadows of those great pieces of iron and stone that stood for all the nameless people lost at sea, and by the fencing pinned with the family photos of the September 11 victims – that the sense of loss and sadness became overpowering.

A life can seem brittle and small, precarious and precious – realising and understanding that is no bad thing. Sometimes, though, it's a matter of working out what's a different perspective and what's just a matter of getting something wrong. Sometimes it can take ten years.

I thought of that morning now, as I stood in front of Kensington Palace. It wasn't much of a palace, really, just a big square house. But I supposed that's what a palace is: someone's big house. It was a beautiful day and as I took in the gates with their floral wreaths I suddenly thought of all those roadside tributes that are dotted around Australia. Little crosses and bunches of flowers, signs of remembrance for those whose lives have been taken in a traffic accident.

When, I thought, did those things start to pop up? Those little bunches of flowers by the roadside are an attempt to say that those lost lives mattered, that they belonged to people who were loved, people who died away from home.

Sarah asked me if I was all right, I said I was. I tried to tell her about what I was thinking, about how this big fence with its dying flowers didn't seem to mean as much.

'Maybe it's because it's … sort of all English,' I said. I gestured to the Hobbytex portrait of Princess Diana.

'God, you are a boofhead sometimes,' said Sarah. 'Have you seen where it's from?'

'From England. It's from somewhere in England.'

'Yeah?'

I humphed and then crouched down and read the poem and who wrote it and from where it had been sent.

Princess Diana = princess of hearts
When you left us
We fell apart
Why did they take you?
Why was it so?
Gone but not forgotten –
You loved your sons so

Angel of goodness, mother who loved
Now smile shyly from heaven above.
Sadly missed.
From Don and Carol Werribee, South Victoria, Australia

Don and Carol. Good on them.

'Where might Don and Carol come from?' said Sarah.

'Well, they might be English migrants,' I mumbled and we walked on through the park.

We held hands and I felt sad. Not sad that a rich person from a big house had died; I didn't care about her being a princess, in fact I couldn't give a rat's arse. Perhaps that was what I had reacted to all those years ago, with the self-important news presenter and his death-of-Diana moment. I was sad that she had died so far from home, sad that her children would be without her. It was as sad as the lives lost at sea, the lives remembered by the roadside shrines in Australia, the lives lost in New York that September morning. It was a life lost.

I held Sarah's hand and thought that I'd learnt a little something.

'Fuck, I love you,' I suddenly blurted.

'You are so romantic, Will,' Sarah said, but she did give my hand a little squeeze.

There are other ways to get over long-haul flights, and on our trip across the Pacific Clem and I found a beauty.

Jumping in a car driven by a mumbling man who scythed his way through the traffic in an homage to the film *The French Connection*, he would mumble in a language that neither of us understood and the car would lurch and leap across the roads of Los Angeles. This was good because it prepared me for what was to follow: two weeks in LA. Or, to be more precise, two weeks on every conceivable roller coaster and ride in LA. Nothing that I sat in, revolved in, spun in and shook and rattled and rolled in over the next two weeks was as bad as that trip to the hotel, though. No, nothing matched what the *French Connection* cabbie got up to along the freeways of Los Angeles. In fact, I should have handed his business card to the various theme parks that dot the West Coast of America; he'd be a wonderful attraction.

On our itinerary the *French Connection* Experience was delicately termed our 'transfer' from LAX airport to our hotel. In reality, our driver was one of those people thrown up by life whom you meet once and never forget.

'What do you think of America?' I asked Clem as we leapt across the bitumen.

'It's pretty busy,' he said with a straight face and then added, 'They wear a lot of uniforms.'

Indeed they do. It's slightly confronting when you traipse in long lines from a plane to be confronted by so many uniforms in a major American airport. Marines, armed to the teeth, the heavy belted customs officers, the airport police with their slow walks and clunky guns, the airport staff and yes, even the driver of our transfer. He wore a uniform. And a cap. He looked a little like someone from *Star Trek* and for good measure he drove like he was at the controls of the *Enterprise*, at warp speed.

'Well,' I said to Clem, 'there are reasons for so many uniforms.'

The French Connection turned to me and – startlingly – spoke to me in an accent that even *sounded* like it was from *Star Trek*.

'We are at war. We need to protect us!' He smiled and then pointed. 'Your hotel!'

We were indeed at our hotel and before our transfer zoomed off my son looked at me. 'Are they at war? The Americans?'

'Yes,' said the French Connection. 'Yes, with the whole world! Enjoy, enjoy!' He smiled, waved and careered off into the traffic.

We looked at each other; I wondered how Clem would react to what he had just heard.

'Can we go to Disneyland?' he said.

'Fair enough,' I said. He had a sense of perspective. We had flown across the Pacific and this was one of the reasons we were here.

We checked in and were told by our hosts that we still had time to catch some of the continental breakfast, which was a part of our package. Well, there are continental breakfasts and there are continental breakfasts. Perhaps something was lost in the translation. We walked into a room to find a packet of blueberry bagels, some white bread for toasting and some fruit juice. And a sad-faced old woman in a uniform, whose job it was to pour filter coffee and wipe up the spillage.

Clem looked at her and she looked at him. He said hello and she looked at him. He said it again and she nodded and said, 'Hello, sir.'

Clem blanched.

We had our blueberry bagel, filter-coffee breakfast, and the woman wiped up some coffee stains that weren't there. We said 'Thank you' and Clem smiled. The lady stared ahead.

Later, Clem and I walked down the wide, dry avenues of Anaheim towards Disneyland. On our way we passed a market garden run by a Japanese–American family. We stopped and bought a punnet of strawberries, washed them and ate them as we continued on our trek.

They were fresh and sweet, nearly a little too ripe but full of flavour. We passed T-shirt shops and bars and restaurants, even an Outback Steakhouse. It was a a resort-lover's dream. A place of 'Lands' and 'Worlds' and all-you-can-eat buffets.

'These strawberries,' Clem said. 'These strawberries are something I will remember.'

They were also the freshest food we would have in the next two weeks.

He smiled at me, munching on the last of the fruit. 'That old lady called me "sir". She didn't have to do that. Was she as old as Nanna Mac?'

'Maybe,' I said.

'As Nanna Anna?'

'Maybe,' I said.

'I don't think it's right she called me "sir",' he said.

More people in uniforms staff Disneyland. This time, with name tags and an additional tag to let people know how long they have worked there. One man, who looked older than our continental breakfast overseer, had a tag that informed us he had twenty-seven years' service at Disneyland. He wore a boater at a jaunty angle and smiled a lot.

'You've picked a good time to come to Disneyland, it's in between our holiday break and when lots of you folks from overseas come. You won't have to wait for the attractions.'

He seemed genuinely happy for us. He loved Disneyland, loved being there and meeting people. 'You Aussies and the folks from Ireland are my favourites, you know,' he said as he waved us on our way.

What I found slightly disturbing was that his manner was that of a teenager but his age was closer to that of a pensioner. Oh well.

It seemed the second week of January is the time to go to Disneyland. We didn't need to wait long for rides, though that was something of a mixed blessing. It meant I could go in a collapsing hotel lift that plummeted four floors and reared itself up again as often as I liked or, to be more precise, as often as my Clem liked.

I had payback, insisting we had photos taken with all the characters we saw, and he complied. To my astonishment he was taller than almost every costumed character, towering over Mickey and Donald and even Goofy. He was growing up.

So I made him come on the teacups and saucers.

'I have to go on these, Clem. I used to think these things were unobtainable. Every Sunday night on the telly I would see them.'

He was a good boy and understood that his father needed some time for the fulfilment of a passing childhood fancy. The teacups and saucers.

Then we went on the river plunge again.

There were so many theme parks and lands to visit!

The glorious ridiculousness of southern California is the way in which any theme, any morsel of history, can be packaged and Americanised to entertain and earn a dollar. No nation is safe. We experienced an insanely entertaining night at Medieval Times. A night of jousting, falconry and revelry.

We sat in a big arena on long benches and were given plastic tankards and plates. A young woman, sounding like someone from the television show 'Glee', informed us she was Tamara and our 'wench' for the night and she would like to remind us that her gratuities are not included in our admission.

Tipping! Tipping; even here in medieval times it rears its head. What do they say? Ten per cent of what you pay.

'Oh,' added Tamara, 'please don't bang your balls and plates as it disturbs the horses.'

Clem and I looked at each other.

'What did she say?' said Clem.

'I think it's her accent and she means "bowls and plates".' We nodded and drank from our plastic mugs.

Thereafter, we were entertained by a group of stuntmen and some truly remarkable acting. It was like watching a 1950s sword-and-shield flick from a wet Saturday afternoon on the telly.

We were advised by a smooth-voiced master of ceremonies – sounding for all the world like he was selling shampoo – to 'Give it up for the Green Knight! My lords and ladies, the *Green Knightttt!*'

They pretended to fight and had a dancing horse and a falcon that couldn't seem to fly straight and at the end we were invited back to meet 'your favourite chivalrous knights for photo opportunities and refreshments at our … knight club'.

Clem could hardly contain himself as we roared with laughter. 'Give it up for the Green Knight' became the mantra for the holiday.

And yes, there was more.

We travelled to Six Flags Magic Mountain, which had a collection of roller coasters and rides on which NASA trains its astronauts. Well, I don't know if they actually do, but they should. It was a little like a primal form of shock treatment, with many magic words uttered and screamed as human bodies were pushed this way and that. It was an oddly bonding experience to be scared utterly senseless, sharing this with complete strangers.

Clem managed to lose a hat and a camera and I yelled at him. It was just like home. I sometimes wonder why I yell at him so much and I made a vow to myself in the cab back to the hotel to try not to yell at him so often. I went into Thinking Father 101 mode and decided to give him a bit of responsibility.

The next day we ate a continental breakfast with the old lady, who was as unsmiling as ever.

'Clem,' I said. 'Clem, I'm going to give you this ticket to SeaWorld. It's your ticket, you have to look after it.'

He nodded and said he would. He said thank you.

I told him it was all right and Clem told me he was thanking the old lady.

I said, 'Good boy.'

I turned to her, too, and said, 'Thank you.'

The old lady looked at Clem and said, 'Thank you, sir.'

SeaWorld is in San Diego and as we travelled there we passed a huge naval base, which apparently specialised in landing craft. A sign towered over the entrance that proclaimed 'No Beach is Out of Our Reach'. Clem looked at the base and then to me and said, 'That's sort of scary. It sounds like they are angry at the whole world, like the French Connection said.'

We got off the bus and I took out my ticket. Clem looked at me.

I looked at him.

He looked away from me.

'Where's your ticket?'

He looked at me and said quietly, 'Give it up for the Green Knight.'

I went into Exploding Father Outrage 101 mode and sent him to the other side of the car park.

He yelled back to me, 'I'm sorry for losing my ticket!'

I didn't say anything.

He continued, 'Why do I have to stand over here?'

From the other side of the car park he looked very small. Even so I still yelled, 'Because I don't want to bloody strangle you!'

Some people stopped and stared a bit and then walked on.

Amazingly, he yelled back, 'Fair enough, Daddy.'

I calmed down and yelled out, 'Give it up for the Green Knight!' and he came over. He'd been crying. I said I was sorry and he held my hand.

He told me he was sorrier so I promised not to yell at him ever again. He just laughed.

Inside SeaWorld we saw the famous Shamu the killer whale's show, 'Believe'. But before we did, we stood for a minute in honour of 'Our fighting men and women and their allies who defend freedom and our way of life.'

Now, hearing words like these is slightly surreal in this part of the land, where everything is made up along theme-park lines. But Americans are nothing if not literal. They commit to what is said and I doubt if there is any room for irony. So we stood in honour and then a man with a microphone popped out and said, 'Do you wanna see Shamu?'

The crowd roared back.

'I don't think he can hear youuuuuuuu! Do youuuu wannaaaa seeeeeee Shamuuuuuuuu?'

We sure do!

I knew I did and I went a little Shamu crazy. I saw a terrific spot under some floodlights and hauled Clem along with me.

'Dad!' he said.

'Come on!' I said. 'We can get a good look at Shamu.'

'Dad …' He looked doubtful.

'Come on, Clemmy, I want to see Shamu.'

A part of me realised I sounded like a lunatic but *I wanna see Shamuuuuuuuuuu!*

We saw Shamu do his stuff. And I got shat on by about two hundred seagulls that parked their arses over the edge of the floodlights. I had more bird crap on me than was ever mined on Nauru. The crowd went ape for Shamu and Clem nearly wet himself laughing.

I decided to take Clem to downtown LA, a place of Latino wedding shops, bargain basements and glary neon-fronted retailers. Every once in a while there were clumps of bodies lying in doorways, sleeping across the pavement.

We ate at the central markets, a place seldom seen on the tourist listings and where everything is rough and ready. My son looked around and chose a meal. A man sitting at a table close by smiled. 'Pretty good that food, huh?' he said.

Clem smiled back. He was hungry my boy, I could tell. He ate the chop suey and suddenly slowed. He looked across at the man at the table.

'It's good,' my son said.

'Yes,' said the man.

Clem looked at me. And then back at the man at the table nearby. 'But I'm full.'

'Mind if I …' the man trailed off.

My son smiled and handed over his plate. The man ate the food quickly.

As we walked away I realised that I hadn't even noticed the man was hungry.

'I wish we could give him some of those strawberries from that farm … This place has so much and he has so little … It is funny, I think. I wish that old lady hadn't called me "sir",' Clem said.

We walked together, Clem and I, and I put an arm around his shoulder.

Three Babies: Stella

Sarah

William's ambitions were not entirely met working at 'Blue Heelers' day after day, week after week. But he knew – or was reminded often enough – that it beat cleaning toilets and he was learning a lot about acting.

He had always seen himself as being an actor like Alec Guinness, though perhaps even he would be too contemporary – more Ralph Richardson or Cary Grant or Laurence Olivier. I think this is because William's idea of contemporary culture is a good thirty or forty years behind that of the rest of us. He can name anyone from virtually any film pre-1980, whether it be actor or director; he could probably even remember the continuity girl.

He 'remembers' quite clearly many things that happened when he was a kid or quite often before he was born; a small detail that doesn't bother him. In politics he has kept up, easily recalling the state member for virtually any seat in any state. But ask him who Rihanna is, or Robert Pattinson or about the benefits of Facebook or the poetry in rap music and he's in trouble. The other day he was looking for the 'wireless'. He calls men 'fellows' or even 'old cock' and signs off a phone call with 'Hooroo!'

He managed to make it through drama school, get an agent and find work in modern plays and television shows seemingly without any of that contemporary knowledge sticking. He doesn't love Dean Martin because he's retro and cool, he just loves Dean Martin. And Al Martino. And Val Doonican.

It did seem unlikely that he would have the career of Alec Guinness or Ralph Richardson or even Cary Grant while spending his days in Mount Thomas police station locking up the locals, no matter how high the crime rate. But then again, it was a job – doing what he liked doing – and it payed the mortgage, too. How many people get that? Spoilt!

I guess I've never really had a true understanding of high ambition. I grew up with a 'women are cooks, men are chefs' mentality. When art was the only subject I could scrape a pass in, it was suggested I become an art teacher, though I wasn't a fan of school or bells. And though I knew there were such people as artists, not just art teachers, they usually seemed to be men or those rare women who knew what to do and thought that things were achievable. It took me a good twenty years to get a handle on such an outlook.

I did do drama when I was younger. My parents sent me to a Saturday morning theatre group, mostly to cure my outside-the-home shyness and give voice to my inside-the-home dramatics.

After a few years of being the lighting girl, the prompt or the follow-spot operator with occasional stints as a serving girl in between, we were visited by a community theatre guru and I, along with a couple of other non-stars, followed him to a new youth theatre in Carlton. This eventually led me, at age eighteen, to be in a Theatre in Education team that toured rural areas as well as metropolitan Melbourne in a bashed-up Kombi van with homemade props.

We also had a space, in Carlton, now part of Safeway, where we put on pretty diverse theatrical material, anything from Brecht to rolling around on black plastic. In one performance I was required to be up a ladder for an hour and a half giving birth. I can't remember to what. My first starring role was as Badjelly in Spike Milligan's *Badjelly the Witch*.

Our patron at the theatre was Glenda Jackson, at the time one of the great English actresses, now a great English politician. She was in Australia touring with a play, when she came to the theatre. She loved it – the energy, the youth, the idea of a 'poor theatre', a youth theatre bringing drama to life, making it accessible, political and socially relevant.

I decided to go overseas at age nineteen, telling everyone I wanted to see the world, visit the great art galleries and museums and watch great theatre, but in reality I wanted to follow my current boyfriend. The director of our company wrote to Glenda saying I was coming, asking whether she would look after me, show me the ropes and give me some introductions. She was my only contact in Europe – apart from the object of my affections, who in hindsight was perfectly happy to be travelling on his own, sending me only the odd postcard.

I worked in three separate hospitals at the same time to earn my plane fare: two aged-care homes and one psych hospital. I read an out-of-date book about travelling around Europe on ten dollars a day, thought I could do it for a bit less and didn't take inflation into account. And never mind that it would be winter.

We didn't hear back from Glenda before I left, not unusual in those days of airmail letters on that tissue-thin blue paper that formed an envelope. It hadn't been long since we had sent the letter – a mere couple of weeks – but with me in a panic, the director probably blew her life savings and stayed up until midnight to make a call to London, where Glenda's colleagues were apologetic that her reply hadn't reached us, were sure she would have replied and were also sure she wanted to meet me. They gave out the address and advised me to just turn up.

They were sure she wanted to meet me – people always say that when they have no idea, they were obviously just being polite. They didn't even know if she'd received the letter. She may not have. Or she may have tossed it in the bin, sick of desperate youths from all over the world coming to sit dumbly in her office, wasting her time. For heaven's sake, what was she meant to do with them? Wasn't being a patron to these cultureless try-hard colonials enough?

I got on the plane, like so many before me and since, and had maybe one of the most comfortable nights of my entire trip; with a whole row to myself, people bringing me food, a blanket and wine, though these were the days of smoking on planes, so we all inhaled, whether or not we lit up ourselves.

Once installed in the cheapest backpackers' I could find, I went to the address I had been given for Glenda. I walked up to the door, paused, then walked away again. What was I supposed to say? Who was I to ask for? It was an office, not a home. Of course. As if she'd expect me at her house! But what about the office? Would they have heard of me? Would they think I was of the same mental state as the patients I was used to cleaning around, thinking they were Jesus?

I didn't knock.

I went to the address again the next day, and many days after that. I would walk past repeatedly, rehearsing my entrance and what I'd say, then lose faith, wander around aimlessly and go back to the hostel to wish I was someone else. I couldn't decide what to wear, what to say, when would be the best time of day. Once, I walked right up and opened the door, but when the person inside – who was on the phone – gestured for me to wait, I lost my nerve and left.

I fled England for the cheaper and warmer countries of southern Europe and northern Africa. I didn't have enough money to get into most of the galleries and museums or for a *paella* in Spain or even to go to Venice, but was rewarded with many other adventures, although admittedly some took ten years of reminiscing to become more than just horrible experiences.

I had sold everything I owned and had no more money, hadn't heard from anyone at home and was lonely, the sometimes-company of the boyfriend not enough to keep me travelling.

So I went back to London and to the post office. The first letter I opened, in my mother's hand, was a Christmas card from months before and some money fell out of the envelope. I don't know whether I was more thrilled she hadn't forgotten me or that I had money to buy something to eat. I went straight to the nearest pub, found a corner booth, dumped my tattered bags around me and read through the rest of the mail.

I tried not to cry as I read the letters from family and friends, drawn back towards home and away from travelling. Then I opened one from the theatre company director. Enclosed was the Glenda Jackson letter. She was expecting me. She wanted to introduce me to some people, some theatre people. She would be in London for a few months then in Cornwall making a film. Maybe, if I was interested in film, she could introduce me to the people creating it? Then a note from the theatre director. Glenda had apparently also called, worried when I hadn't shown up, repeating her enthusiasm to have someone from the company visit London. I looked at the date. She was already in Cornwall.

I put my head on the table. Should I go to the office? Should I go to Cornwall? Was I the kind of person who could do that? I had been hungry and cold for six months, but was still chubby. I had no clean clothes. And if I did go, then what? If I couldn't even knock on the door, how could I ever do an audition? I was never going to meet Glenda Jackson never mind *be* Glenda Jackson. I had another cider and caught the plane home, leaving my theatrical ambitions behind. In my family, we now call it 'doing a Glenda Jackson'; ruining something all by yourself.

This experience didn't put me off enjoying the fruits of others' work, though. I've always loved most British acting, my favourite aspect being the quality of the performance in the minor roles in both films and television series. Even characters without lines seem able to lift a scene and make it believable, authentic and keep you glued to the narrative. A scene where the lead guy buys cigarettes is only as good as the shopkeeper's performance, never just the lead guy's.

Maybe it was a combination of my failure and a great respect for RADA graduates that made me want to support William in his ambition some years later. And to fulfil his ambition we probably needed to go to Britain or the US. William could work in Britain, his parents having been born there, and making it in Britain also seemed the best way for an Australian actor to get to Hollywood. And Hollywood, of course, is the creative centre of the world's film and TV culture, if 'culture' is the right word.

We allow it to be so, here in Australia. We love our own music and authors, our own sporting codes, our own beer and wine and we don't particularly care what anyone else in the world thinks. But our films? No. Our scriptwriters? No. Much of our TV? No. When it comes to the arts, it has to be validated by either Britain or America first, before we allow ourselves to see merit.

We can be very supportive of Australianness so it is sad that we are, as a nation, 'doing a Glenda Jackson', and potentially will be left with no Australian identity in film and TV, the most accessed form of entertainment and art we have.

We decided to go, though, just so William could come home again eventually and have a better chance of a career here. We only had one baby and a mortgaged house that we could sell. We did the sums, made the plans, gritted our teeth and – didn't go.

My father got sick and 'Blue Heelers' offered William a brand new and improved contract. We paused. We thought.

Fathers getting sick had got in our way before. We had attempted to get married after we had Cosmo. Twice we tried, sending invitations and planning where and what, with William's father Colin having a crisis on the first date and dying just before the second. William was there when his father went downhill fast after a long, slow decline and then when he died. He was pleased he had been there and I didn't like the idea of leaving my dad.

We eventually got married without the 'do'. William's mother didn't speak to me for more than a year for having done her out of a 'knees-up'.

My father had cancer, a recurrence of the bowel cancer he'd had a tiff with five years previously. He wouldn't have wanted us to stay in Australia for him; he would have wanted us to believe, as he did, that it would be another little argument with the disease, then situation normal again. But having Clem and losing William's father made us both more focused on family. William was close to my dad. They both liked a cup of tea at the football, leaving the beer for the pub afterwards; a deep outsider bond these days.

The pause allowed William to think about the reality of living and working in Britain. Having been brought up within the wider Britannia Club that is Redcliffe and also deep inside the Britannia Club *in* Redcliffe, William finally confessed he had no real interest in going to Britain. The outposts often seem to maintain the capital 'C' in culture more than in the actual country. He was over Britain. He was not just Australian, he was a Queenslander. And for a cricket-loving Queensland boy, Britain was the arch rival, not home.

One day, when we were taking Clem to irritate Dad, in the way that all young children irritated him, William said to me: 'I'd rather have another baby.'

This surprised me. William was still young, his ambition still in place. Few of his friends had had babies yet and I think considered him to have already betrayed the inner-city groove and arts scene by embracing suburbia. We still had our old Falcon and could find our way to the city, but would this be the end of that, too?

I asked him, 'More than playing Hamlet at Stratford?'

'Yes,' he said.

'More than being charming in something on in the West End?'

'Yes.'

'More than being a baddie in the next breakthrough British film?'

'How do you know I wouldn't get the lead guy?'

'Sorry. More than the lead guy?'

William sighed. 'We could bring the toilet inside if I did "Blue Heelers".' There was a pause. 'And I wouldn't feel like I was sucking up to England.'

True. And for me, I liked our house and the maternal amnesia had kicked in, leaving only the wonderful memories of my arms being full of a chubby, giggling bundle of gorgeousness. And I hated the cold. Melbourne was quite rainy and cold enough for me, and at least it knows how to have a summer. And, even better, how to have an autumn. And a spring. What better sport than trying to guess the weather for the Melbourne Cup?

We decided to stay home and have another baby and hope the giant ants weren't due in Mount Thomas for at least another year.

So I rid myself of the birth control I had reinstated during the first six months of Clem's life, thinking I would never go through that again. Why would I ever, ever, want to do that again? And we started to try. No luck. Then we tried and tried. Nothing except the odd late period and an impossible-to-quench desire to test out the new home pregnancy tests that were on the market. I didn't know then how familiar and depressing those little buggers can be. What are they for? Like dog food, there was once no need for them. You never thought of being pregnant until you missed your second period. Now you can panic because you're not pregnant – or that you are pregnant – within days. Soon, you are buying one every month, then another one in case the first was inconclusive.

My father was, at this time, getting sucked into a parallel medical world. I would be doing tests for the right kind of hormones, he for tumour markers. His happy outcome would be that his results were *down*, mine that the results were *up*. I don't like giving myself over to that realm, but when you are first faced with it, it is very seductive. You don't know why your body is failing you. The doctors think they do, and not only that, they think they can fix it. The trick is just to allow them to do that and not let your whole world become confined to the next appointment or the next test. But it's hard not to as that part of your life becomes so central, so there is a certain pleasure in handing yourself over.

Then, for me, not just a late period but the first little blue line. For Dad, lowered tumour markers. We were go; pregnant and holding.

I did a couple of tests to make sure, then made an appointment at the hospital. But before the appointment an early miscarriage; definitely not a late period, because of the blue lines. Did I need to know that? Did I need to start thinking of those obviously not well-formed cells as a baby, as a child I had lost? I doubt it. Did I learn from that mistake and not buy another pregnancy test the next month? Of course not.

We tried again. Another early miscarriage. Then a pregnancy that was still showing the blue lines strongly into week ten. We went to the hospital. All good. We booked in for the usual tests, got excited, told people and I dug out my old 'fat' tops. Then the ultrasound at seventeen weeks. No baby. The baby had died very early but my body had kept thinking I was pregnant. A phantom pregnancy. A term I thought had gone out with 'having the vapours' or 'the wireless'. But apparently one that is still with us, enough to give me the vapours.

The doctors sent us home from the hospital, saying they didn't know how or why it had happened, that it was a weird mind–body thing. I asked if my body would keep thinking it was pregnant until forty weeks and then give birth to a puff of air and blood that would be our phantom baby. We were told this was doubtful; now that I knew, my body should catch on soon, that they might use a curette if it didn't resolve itself. Start afresh, so to speak.

My body didn't catch on and the doctors used the curette, gave me a good old clean-out. It might have been wise to pause then, maybe go back to having sex when we wanted to, not care about the outcome, just be happy we had Clem.

But, my best and worst trait being stubbornness – inherited from both my parents, each calling the other stubborn, but themselves blessed with accommodating natures – we kept trying to get pregnant. I did shoulder stands on the bedroom floor for half an hour after our duty sex. I inspected mucus, kept an intricate diary, ate bananas, took folic acid, listened to my body and was rewarded with another blue line and another miscarriage. We delved further into the medical world and went to a fertility specialist.

'It's not so much that you can't get pregnant, you don't seem very good at staying pregnant,' he said. 'I can't do much about that, but we can at least make sure you ovulate every month to maximise your chances of one sticking.'

I'm not sure 'sticking' was his word. The medical world tends to use clinical terms like 'viable'.

I'm not a pill-taker. I prefer a glass of wine to a Panadol for a headache. I figure it causes the same damage to my liver and has about the same chance of working. And if you have a second glass, at least you know why you have the headache. But as I had embraced this parallel universe of medicine I took the ovulation pills, and we kept trying. I now bought pregnancy tests in bulk, along with tissues.

William was starting to react to my suggestion we have sex as if I were asking him to look through the rubbish bin for lost car keys. It was hardly a sexy suggestion from me either; the lingerie, oysters and champagne, massages and lipstick long gone, it was now more of a look up from the newspaper or a tired greeting at the door and, 'It's time, we'd better do it, can you manage it?'

William would sigh, a beer or coffee being topmost in his mind.

'Please?'

He would nod and we would slump off to the bedroom, equally unenthusiastic, and do the duty.

We reached our last round of pills and still no viable pregnancy. We were sick of it all. It felt as if I had spent the previous seven years oscillating between some sort of pregnancy or breastfeeding. To continue with Mr Fertility would be to start talking test tubes and small rooms with pornography. William hates pornography. He'd had enough.

I'd had enough. We gave up. Well, William gave up. I'm not sure I did, but I went along with the conversation, believing it at the time.

'Let's have at least six months without thinking of it. A year. Let's have a holiday and drink mango daiquiris. Let's only have sex when we both feel like it. Really *really* feel like it.'

So we booked the holiday with the best happy hour with William's brother and sister-in-law, who had three small children and a great need for a week of cocktails. We bought a bottle of champagne. William raised his glass.

'No more duty sex,' he said.

I touched glasses with him.

'No more pregnancy tests.'

'Promise?'

'I promise,' I said.

William looked at me, not quite trusting me.

'I promise! I swear on whatever you want me to swear on!'

We toasted and in that moment I believed myself.

We drank the champagne and toasted our only child. Our Clem, now a funny, lovely and hyperactive four-year-old; plenty enough for us, we said.

Then, as you do when your gorgeous child falls asleep and you decide to open another bottle for just one more glass, and when there is no way you're ovulating because you had your period only two days earlier, you have sex.

Then the next day we woke up, paid for the holiday and reclaimed our place in the non-medical world.

Life was good. My sisters were back in Melbourne after stints in the country and overseas. As they are two of my best friends, that was a growing pleasure. Dad was holding well. I felt happy.

I played in the garden, I worked. I have always enjoyed working. I love a project. I don't mind that much whether it's painting a picture or a door, paving the backyard or making a film. I just don't like anyone else telling me what hours to work. Left on my own, I'll work long days and love it. And at the end of a project, I love the feeling of completion, the cold beer of satisfaction. Then the tidying before the start of the next project.

It doesn't always matter to me when projects fail. I don't give up easily, but sometimes you have to, either because it's going nowhere or someone offers you actual money to change tack. I have applied for many more jobs than I've ever been given and have a few bottom drawers full of rejected scripts, thousands of photos from unfunded animation projects, half-knitted jumpers.

The baby project now safely in the bottom drawer, I tidied up and got to work, taking on two jobs. The first was directing a short film in live action, something only animators call film-making. It was a funny piece from a script by my friend Leanne, entitled *Derwent Envy*; a look back at the era of our childhoods when sex education was minimal, understanding even less so, and the desire to have a set of Derwent pencils and takeaway on Fridays exceeded all other concerns. It was a pleasure to write while having Clem for company, just as his personality was taking definite shape, his current obsession being a Thomas the Tank Engine T-shirt.

It would have been a great film, except we only received half the funding we needed and instead of waiting and retrying and reworking, we made the oft fatal mistake of deciding that any film was better than none, and chopped the script in half. In such a cutthroat industry, a bad film can be much worse than no film; you have lost your 'potential'.

The other job, which would start the following year, was twelve months directing an animated film for children about migratory birds. This would be the year Clem started school so I would be able to work away from home.

William was also having a few tentative chats about life after his 'Blue Heelers' contract ran out, so he was happy as well. Our life together was as secure as life could be for an actor and animator. We organised a renovation to bring the toilet inside, which, as renovations tend to do, soon involved a proper bathroom, a new kitchen, a study, a new front door and a deck out the back.

I bought tiles, trawled the hard garbage and through junk shops for old windows, bits of handy timber. The builder would sigh, but soon gave up trying to convince me it would cost just as much in the end and went along with it. I felt good, satisfied and a bit sick.

My period didn't arrive when it usually did. I tried not to notice the date. I was on Project Renovation and Project Get Film Up. There was no Project Baby.

I did my best as two weeks went by and still no period. I had been there so many times, I told myself not to think about it. But then I'd throw up. I love the sort of throwing up I do when pregnant; I'd become so good at it I could almost get the bag, vomit into it and tie it off at the traffic lights. But I wasn't pregnant, I'd tell myself firmly and go looking for a basin with taps intact that someone was throwing away.

I didn't tell William. He didn't need these feelings to have to suppress. Life was good; we were going on holiday, we were going to drink cocktails. Cocktails. How can you tell yourself that you aren't pregnant and still hit the happy hour? What if by some tiny little chance you *are*?

It was enough. I went and bought a pregnancy test, snuck it into the house and did it. 'Pregnant' it read. The next day I did it again. 'Pregnant' it read. I did it every day before we caught the plane. Every day, pregnant. I was almost annoyed with the blue lines. The baby obviously wouldn't stick. I was thirty-eight, I'd have another miscarriage yet I wouldn't be able to drink cocktails. Dammit.

We went to the island. I had to tell William. He wasn't about to believe my excuses of being on a diet, just not feeling like it, preferring the mocktails really, wanting to spend time with Clem at cocktail hour. Especially when he saw Clem crying as I tried to drag him from the video that the kids' club was screening. So William drank all my cocktails for me, half in hopeful celebration, half in panic it was going to be another sad outcome.

We came home. Still no period. Eight weeks, ten weeks. I ignored it until twelve weeks, then a tiny hope that maybe this one was going to stick. I had denied myself cocktails. Maybe that was what the gods of desire had required from me, that level of commitment, giving up treats I never normally had.

We went over to see my parents and sat around the dining table, while Clem played on a stool happily in the next room, driving Dad nuts.

My father's levels had climbed a little, but he was clinging to the oncologist's words, 'They can fluctuate.' He had also received advice from his regular golfing partner that the growing pain in his side sounded more like appendicitis than anything sinister. His tone was hopeful, almost pleading. 'Please agree with me.'

I sat there, not knowing what to say, sensing this was the beginning of the pathway that Dad was going to take, and therefore the one I and the rest of the family would also have to take. Stick to the small battles, don't mention the war. Dad looked thinner, older. My innards turned over in a churning wash of sad panic.

'Maybe it is appendicitis?' I said. 'Why not? Or a hernia, or indigestion. No offence, Mum.'

We laughed. Even Mum. William got up and removed Clem from the stool and Dad's eyeline, then wandered off. He was upset and not wanting to show it. I looked after him, wishing I'd bagsed that idea first. What could I say to Dad? Every subject I thought of involved the future. I put another bite of baked chop in my mouth.

Then I felt the most joyful little flutter inside, like bubbles, or butterflies, or giggles given shape. The baby kicking.

Unbelievable. How many times in my life would the good be tempered with the bad? I sat with it for a moment. Then I said to Dad, 'How was golf?'

That night William and I lay mostly silent in bed, him trying to feel the little flutters, me moving his hand to where I thought they would be. We were together in it all. We didn't speak, there was nothing really to say.

I went back to the same hospital, where they put us in the same clinic. I was booked in for the usual tests. I noticed one was missing.

'What about the estriol levels test?' I asked.

The nurse looked vague. 'The what?'

'An estriol level test. I've had it before, and I had low levels.'

The nurse looked through my big fat file.

'Oh yes, that was a trial, not a standard test. We don't need it now.'

'You don't need it?'

'No, the trial finished.'

'But I had low estriol levels, I had vitamins, long-line drips.'

The nurse gave the smallest of shrugs.

'But what if I've still got them? What did the trial find out?'

The shrug was a bit bigger now.

I began to speak firmly, but ended tearily. 'I'd just like to know. Seeing as I was part of it, I should know.'

The nurse nodded, expressionless, then stood up and left the room.

I felt embarrassed, needy and demanding. But it didn't make sense to me. This was the medical world. Things didn't just disappear.

The nurse was gone for a long while. I sat and waited in the cubicle. I'd sat in a few by then. There was never anything personal in the rooms, just posters and warnings: 'Always wash your hands'; 'Stop! Tell the X-ray technician if you think you could be pregnant'.

The cubicles were used by different doctors dealing with different things each day. Clinics for this and that. Today, 'Yes, your pregnancy is going well; height good, weight good, see you next month.' Tomorrow, 'Your tumour markers are a bit lower. It could be bad news, but they can fluctuate. We'll see where we are in a month.'

Finally, the nurse came back in with a young registrar.

'The trial is finished,' he said, then repeated himself as I was obviously an idiot. 'It's finished, the results were inconclusive. They didn't find a link,' he glanced down at the folder he had dug out of the archives. 'No proven link. Low estriol levels are not related to low-birth-weight babies or babies with problems,' he read. He looked back at me and enunciated clearly. 'So no test. No need to test. Good news. No test.'

Apparently, when you question some areas of medicine you must be an idiot. And I guess I felt like one.

I went home, still stunned. The trial had been for nothing. If we hadn't been in the trial they wouldn't have induced me early with Cosmo. The trial was why we lost Cosmo. Losing Cosmo was for nothing. I cried.

Unable to have a stiff drink, I had a bath in the nearly finished bathroom, the old anger swirling in me. The grief had softened, but the anger never really went away. No

one at the hospital had said sorry when we lost Cosmo. They had all avoided that word so neatly and carefully it was easy to see they cared more about admitting fault than our feelings. It was a public hospital and we weren't the litigious types. I don't like the way the world is changing just to avoid lawsuits and I still pride myself on not taking any legal action, though the hospital changed its rules because of us. Now all induced babies are monitored during labour. But there was nothing to be gained for us. We had lost Cosmo. We hadn't lost money, he wasn't damaged and in need of special care, he was just dead. All I wanted was for them to say sorry. Sorry, sorry, sorry.

As I lay there in an indulgent amount of water, I tried to quell the anger. I find anger is a bad thing to hold on to and difficult to expunge. Although tears come easily to my eyes, I've never been a good cryer. Even when I'm alone I feel faintly ridiculous after the first few sobs. The one time uncontrollable hysteria took over and I couldn't stop making the weirdest noises in my parents' bathroom, was months after Cosmo died. My sister's baby was crying and I hadn't particularly registered it until my sister, tears in her eyes, turned to me and said, 'Sorry, sorry, I can't make her stop. Sorry.'

I ran from the room as if I was going to throw up, leant over the basin and vomited the sobs instead.

Now, I looked at the patterns that were playing with the light from the old hibiscus tree outside. Through the new and trendy glass bricks, each one looked like a small expressionist painting. I had filled my small world with greens and creams. No angry colours. I began to count what I had. Not my blessings, just what I had: a car, a healthy child, a lovely man, enough money to pay the mortgage, not enough to cause worry, Australian citizenship, ten pairs of shoes. A pathetic amount in some eyes, absurdly wasteful in others.

I had taught myself to do this. I was trying to make myself a positive person. I wanted that glass half-full, no matter how much unfairness in the world, how many starving people, global catastrophes or prophecies of doom.

I wanted to hear the voice of promise and hope and optimism. I wanted to not just know that birth and death are inevitable, but to believe it, to allow for it, to be at peace with it.

Doing this, I can soon build myself up to feeling so lucky, which, once diluted with the extraordinary amount of self-pity I can hold, leaves me in a place of confused and teary but functional neutrality.

Of course it's not always good to lie in the bath and count what you have. If you're having a particularly good run in life, it can be scary. Everything's going well, clearly, the house will now burn down.

This calms the anger. As does trying to see my story from the other side: harassed junior doctors on the thirteenth hour of their twelve-hour shift. Still learning, but already being told never to show that. Communication with nurses too random, a nurse being made to go for tea at the wrong moment. A lack of machinery in the hospital to cope with the number of beds. The continual underfunding of our hospital system through the inability of governments to view their bureaucracies objectively, to see them for the monsters they can become. Well, maybe thinking this way doesn't completely quash the anger, but it certainly redirects it down less agressive paths, like the one that makes people write letters to the paper.

Regret can be harder for me to shake. Counting the things I have doesn't silence that voice, sometimes quiet, sometimes physically painful, that says 'If only.' If only I had chosen the Thursday clinic not the Tuesday clinic to have my baby. If only the woman in the next bed hadn't been having twins and needed the monitor. If only the car had broken down on the way, so they would have delayed for a week and Cosmo's head would have properly engaged.

How long will I punish myself in this way? How do you rewind to find the moment you made the definitive 'wrong decision'? And if you could, how do you know the other decision wouldn't have been worse? How do you know what is good luck and what is bad luck? What looks like one at the time can often turn out to be the other. Maybe medical science would pay me back one day. It was already doing its best to keep my dad alive. And there had been valuable things to learn from losing Cosmo. William and I were better friends, and probably better parents than we would have been without that wake-up call. We don't take a lot for granted, we recognise the fragility of life, and the need to enjoy what we have when we have it. But were such lessons enough to make it worth losing him? I don't think so.

I was left unsure as to how we should deal with the situation. Should we prepare for this new baby? This doesn't-matter-what-your-estriol-levels-are baby. Or should we do what we did with Clem – nothing – and not jinx our luck. Or would that be jinxing ourselves?

William and I sat on the edge of the bed, pondering this. He gave me a hug, and we held on to it. Clem came in.

'What are you doing out of bed?' we said in unison.

Clem looked at us. 'Give me back that hug,' he said. He climbed up onto us and we had a three-way hug, Clem somewhere near my by now rather obvious belly.

'Is there a baby in your tummy like in Suzzane's tummy?'

William and I looked at each other, then back at Clem. 'Yes,' we said, in unison again.

'Where will it sleep? What will we call it? Will it take my toys? Can I have a brother?'

We were obviously going to have to declare and prepare and take our chances with the fates.

The renovation continued and I walked on the beach again, my pregnant dreaming time. Over the years I had often picked up fragments of glass, attracted by their colour and their dual role of decoration and litter. It didn't seem right to take home the shells – a natural part of the ocean – whereas I could justify removing the manmade glass. Washed, smoothed and softened for years by the sea, the pieces are almost opaque to seem at one with their surroundings.

Inspired, I decided to use these pieces in one of the uglier plain windows I had found – one that would look out over our neighbours' just-as-ugly unpaintable side wall. It would let the light in through the muted sea-glass colours at the same time as making what I hoped would be a beautiful souvenir of the many different beaches I had walked when pregnant with my babies. A worthwhile project that would make it even harder for us to ever leave our house.

I had all the usual tests, plus a few more now that I was older. Although there was much angst and anxiety over their real meaning, all came in with good results, including, after we had asked not to be told, the news that 'she' was a big baby, well into the healthy weight bracket.

And so our baby girl grew inside me, her strong kicking undermining the fragility of her pre-birth state. And as she grew, so did my father's test levels.

Dad wasn't fragile. He'd never really been sick and had no other health problems. The cancer was going to have to work hard to get him. He was sixty-seven, fit, had never smoked or drank much. I only recall him having too many once – not because of any slurring of words or staggering, but by watching him, seemingly sober, standing on the chair in the living room quoting the poetry he remembered learning by rote at school. *Turned back, turned back, by reef and shoal, twin guards of the narrow gate…* until Mum enticed him down with a double serve of his favourite dessert, pavlova.

Dad was having chemotherapy and – because the doctors drill you so thoroughly about what to be careful of and what to avoid – he didn't want anyone coming round if they had the slightest trace of a cold.

I was directing the live-action film *Derwent Envy*, complete with my eight-month frontal blimp, so I couldn't spend time with Dad during the day, and I'd have to wait until William came home from 'Blue Heelers' to go and see him, as Clem seemed to bring home a new cold each week from school.

Maybe I was tired and hot, but I was cross with Dad. Why worry about getting a cold when you have an incurable disease? I didn't get it. Why wouldn't you want to see your grandchildren, have them tumbling about you in the bed, laugh with them and damn the colds? But I supposed that would never have happened, because of the irritation factor of all small children. Dad really only came into his own when they started school or could caddy for him.

As my father's little aliens – his tumours – and my little alien – my daughter – grew bigger, our visits to the doctor changed to every two weeks instead of each month. We were both living in the medical world. We both marked our time by dates, appointments, results and medical opinions. We still didn't talk about the war, or wars, just the results of the skirmishes and war-zone incidents. We ignored the fact that one of us was facing birth and the other, death. A passage into life and a passage out. Me with all the friendly chat and pats from strangers that pregnancy bestowed, him with the awkward silences and withdrawl of people who think dying is already death.

One day Dad went to see his oncologist and the oncologist told him there was nothing more he could do. The chemo wasn't holding the cancer at bay, and there was nothing else to throw at it. Dad was in the terminal stage of the disease. My mother said he seemed to take it well. I think maybe he grasped the word 'stage', and as there are various stages, all of which sound grim, that was as far as he went.

He took it well until they went out to the receptionist, where Dad pulled out his bankcard as usual and asked when the next appointment would be.

'There isn't one,' explained the receptionist. 'There's no need to come back. No point.'

'What, he doesn't want to see me? Not to see how I'm going? To help me through it?'

'That's not really his job,' she replied, I hope embarrassed.

Mum took Dad home, Dad finally depressed.

Dad was still stunned the next time I managed to get over to his house. 'He doesn't want to see me. There's no point,' he repeated to me. 'No point. I thought he liked me. I thought we got on.'

The medical world had seemingly rejected him, while he was still alive and kicking. He had taken on treatment like a job. It was like being retrenched all over again.

Dad had tried from the start to take his prognosis on the chin, but I think he was ill-prepared. Both his parents had lived into their late eighties and he was rarely sick. I don't know where he stood in relation to belief in God, we didn't talk about that. I suspect he did not have a lot of faith. But foretold death leaves you with many large holes and religion can be quick to fill a vacuum. I don't know whether he was just the first to offer his services or whether Dad had sought him out, but my father began a long dialogue with a Buddhist man someone had recommended.

Having been bought up as a vague Presbyterian, hard benches and stoicism its key tenets, this seemed a strange choice. But not being good at belief myself, I had no problem with his decision. I *did* have a problem with the messenger though. He would secrete himself away with Dad for hours, Dad emerging not armed for the future and determined to enjoy the present, but resigned, more depressed than ever and wishing this bloody life would be over so he could move on to the next one.

I don't like the idea of coming back as something else. What could I possibly come back as that would top the life I have? Personally untouched by war or famine, racism or torture, with not only enough to eat, but too much of arguably the best and most diverse cuisines in the world. I have my own room. Maybe all the time spent in the bath counting the good things was beginning to work. I felt so rich that I'd obviously be sent back to the start in a new life and be some cold cellular amoeba at the bottom of a lake or a battery chicken. Even if I came back as a human I'd probably be a Middle Ages slave who dies in the battle paddock over the course of two weeks without painkillers, in the rain.

Dad was still up and about, but didn't leave the house much. Often, he would be lying on the bed when I visited. It was difficult to talk. When you can't mention the future and your fallback conversation is 'Let's go on a holiday', it can be tricky. I regret now not getting out the photo albums and reliving some of the past with him, but if I'm honest I don't think he would have liked it. That, too, would have depressed him.

We didn't talk much of death – it felt presumptuous as a daughter to begin the conversation, though I tried sometimes to let him talk if he wanted to. But we weren't good at it. We had never really talked about Cosmo, my biggest grief to date. I think he knew how I felt and also felt it himself. He had put his arm around me as we walked from the hospital after the funeral. He had come to visit me in hospital, which he normally avoided at all costs. He had never been in one himself as a patient, until he went to the hospice for what would be his last week. My mother was unable to help him to the toilet any more and he refused to allow her or any of us to help him. It was too undignified for him.

I remember seeing a man desperately trying to sell swimming pool pumps at the Royal Show once. He wasn't doing well and looked humiliated. The hall was a mess of noise and showbags, inconsiderate teenagers and rude indifference. For a moment my father reminded me of him. I felt sick.

We went to the hospital to have the baby when the time came.

The same set-up as for Clem – William and I in the room; this time my mother was elsewhere within the hospital, waiting. She never wanted to receive another call like the one she had had from William about Cosmo. And she never wanted to take that long tram journey in to see us. She wanted to be there whatever.

Our big, chubby, gorgeous daughter was born. Again to tears of joy. We named her Stella Marian Lawson McInnes. Stella for no good reason, Marian for my mother's mother and Lawson for my father's mother, but also because she was my third little explorer.

She lay on my chest and I looked at her and I wasn't petrified. Even when her breathing became laboured and the doctor said, casually but firmly, 'That baby needs some help,' and they took her away, I knew it would be all right. She and I had bonded when she was still inside, and as I looked at her then I knew it would be the same outside. And it is. She is still my lovely, lovely girl.

We brought her home on a day of forty-four degrees, the house still in mid-renovation. There were no floorboards in the bedroom, no kitchen to speak of and six men working, installing heating and reblocking. Chaos. But Clem and Iris, his Nanny Mac, had made a sign that hung over the not-yet-complete front door.

Welcome home Sarah and Stella Marian.

Stella was a completely different bundle from Clem. Because I was a different mother? Slightly experienced? Lucky? I don't know. She was placid, cuddly, patient and she slept.

Dad held her. He studied her closely and laughed. 'She's the spit of you!' he said to me. 'Good luck.'

There was love and pride in his words, but mostly a reminder of our tumultuous time when my placid childhood had turned into an outraged adolescence, which had collided nastily with his mid-life crisis. We both eventually emerged and became close, but there were a few questions we never posed and never answered, because that's not how we functioned. The carpet beneath was lumpy from the amount swept under. But who's to say everything must be resolved?

Would Stella and I have a similar collision? Would she have a dream where I dive off the top tower of the pool and hit my head on the other side? Would it be so graphic that she would wake and think she wants me dead? And then feel guilty forever that she was subconsciously an evil person. As I had for many years. I never thought that it might be a love dream and that I cared about my dad, but now I can.

At the same time as looking forward to his next life, Dad had also embraced thinking positively. Thinking positively isn't always a good thing when you're in the terminal stage of cancer. It leaves the superannuation forms unsigned, the Will not written, the 'I love you's unsaid. But it's hard to avoid, this desire to be positive; right from the start you're informed in many and varied ways that you brought this cancer on yourself. Unless it can be directly attributed to smoking or being a Navy plumber in the forties, your cancer is obviously caused by some kind of personality fault. So all you have to do is turn your mind around to fix yourself. And maybe deny yourself all pleasures and just drink veggie juice, preferably something you don't like, to make sure you are punishing yourself severely enough to create a cure. Chemo and radiation don't count, you have to be in charge of it yourself. It's your mind. You have the power. And when to stop that? When do you give up? How do you go from that to graceful acceptance and tidying of affairs?

Dad never wanted to discuss having a funeral, that sort of talk would obviously bring one on. He never left anything specifically to anyone. No instructions either, no passing on of hard-earned wisdom. But one day, as he lay in bed, unable to sit up any longer, when my mother demanded that he at least try to imagine being dead, and could he please advise whether he wanted to be buried or cremated, he replied, 'Cremated. I don't want to be in a box. And put my ashes in the sea with Cosmo. Off the pier.' He looked at me. 'I'll keep him company.'

I doubt I've ever felt so loved and so devastated at the same time. I miss him to this day.

Dad died, and we were thankful his pain, both mental and physical, was over. We took his ashes to the pier, all the family. Stella in a pram, Clem doing his best but failing to focus on Pop rather than the fishermen. And we each scattered a little of Dad into the water. And, like before, we all watched the water, its patterns interrupted momentarily by the ashes before continuing its usual endless rhythms and repetitive cycles.

But we didn't scatter all of him. Mum kept some of his ashes to be with her, to bury under his favourite rose bush, beginning a practice in our family of dividing people up. I like it. We are individuals and mean different things to different people.

A year later, Stella walked down the pier herself as we went to say hello to Pop and Cosmo and, like before, dropped something into the water, a little gift to say hello. This time, one of my dad's favourite roses. It didn't sink or float away, just drifted idly around the pylons, its colours reflecting in the patterns of the water.

Someone on the other side of the pier caught a fish and we went to inspect the catch and admire the deft expertise of the real fishing people. It was a squid, a strange and lovely creature. I thought of it doing the squid swim above any fragment that may be left in this place of my father and my son. I was happy if there were, but if they had been swirled and drifted and were now forming a coral reef or being part of a sandcastle that would wash away on the new tide, it didn't matter either. There was still a part of them in me as well.

Some new people strolled up the pier and looked over the railing and down at the water, as people always do.

'Look at that, a rose.' They watched the yellow–pink flower drift for a moment. 'There must be a story there,' the woman said.

'Lots of stories here,' the man replied, looking at the aged pylons, the scarred woodwork, the historical landing. He glanced at me, staring at them.

I nodded in agreement and apology. Yes lots of stories, then looked away.

We walked back down the pier, our little family of four: father, son, mother, daughter, the full cliché. Happy, grateful and with enough money and time to get ice-creams before we drove to our home. Which we did.

Friends

William

Driving along the Hume Highway, a black cloud of locusts descended from nowhere, turning the passing countryside into a heaving Impressionist landscape. I pulled the car over and waited for the swarm to pass.

My friend Leon stared at the locusts.

'Right from the Bible,' he said. 'Or some poor bloody farmer's wheat crop.'

A suitably awed silence followed, which suddenly broke with us both singing an out-of-tune shocker from the seventies, 'Rubber Bullets' by 10cc.

10cc and biblical locusts. How had it come to this?

The Ratman started it.

The Ratman is a friend who'd invited us to an arts festival in the Upper Murray border country of New South Wales and Victoria; The Weekend of Wonders or, as it's officially known, WOW.

I couldn't resist, because to know the Ratman is to know high adventure in a mundanely eccentric way. He's lived a life, all right. Among the highlights: accruing enough money to purchase a Sydney Harbour ferry to house a floating circus, and then losing enough to have to sell it to some half-baked, would-be L. Ron Hubbard, of Scientology fame, as a floating temple-cum-brothel.

'The circus and the temple never happened,' said the Ratman. 'And the brothel! I reckon the brothel was what the Ron wannabe was really after. Too bad for him. Ferry ended up as scrap. But it's the dream that counts.'

The Ratman is big on dreams; he's the sort of fellow who has enough dreams to go around for lots of other people, although sometimes people just aren't interested in sharing dreams. Especially Ratman's.

A carpenter and builder, the Ratman is also a self-taught musician and bard, who'll turn up anywhere and any time to bung on a show. Sometimes it's at an aged-care facility.

'Some of those oldies really appreciate these songs. Old sweet songs. They don't get the chance to hear them sung by a real person. By me.'

The only problem with the warbling Ratman is that on some occasions he just doesn't stop and his songs have a tendency to bleed together, finally coagulating into a performance that lasts longer than Wagner's *Ring* cycle.

It's not unknown for him to lose some of his audience after a while; some simply drift into sleep, while others just drift away out of the hall and back to whatever it is they usually do.

One performance was punctuated by an old man walking in and out of the hall a number of times, each time with the muttered welcome on seeing the Ratman, 'This bugger still going? Must have one of those batteries shoved up his arse.'

But what no one can deny about the Ratman is his enthusiasm for a cause and the belief in his own ability to entertain.

Sometimes maintaining a belief can be hard, though.

The night Mars was closest to the Earth was the night that we burnt the New York city skyline and a flock of old guitars. Out on a property the Ratman used to own, he asked Leon and me if we'd help him empty a shed. We drove down together in Leon's old Vauxhall Consul, which had a tendency to stop for no apparent reason and then rest a while before gurgling into life again. Leon called these occasions Buddhist Moments.

The Ratman liked the sound of that. 'It's good to leave things up to the universe, or whatever you want to call it; the … the thing.'

He was quieter than usual and as we emptied one of the sheds he became quieter still.

The shed was filled with bits and pieces of his life – old scrapbooks and sheets of music, sets that he'd constructed from some of his old performances, including one of the New York skyline and another of the pyramids and Sphinx. All were thrown onto a heaped pile to build a bonfire. He was going to burn them all.

He went quiet for a long time and stared into the fire. He brought out dozens of old guitars and placed them on the fire. The Ratman had gone travelling with the guitars years before. Sometimes to school fetes and town halls, he'd go almost anywhere; teaching people who wanted to learn how to play for a small donation towards an orphanage in India with which the Ratman had somehow become connected.

'Thought it was doing something for somebody. Maybe some of them still play. That'd be nice to think they might still play. Full of bora,' he said softly.

The guitars squealed, almost hissing, and then some of the strings twanged as they burnt.

'Good fire,' I said.

'It's just a fire to you fellas but I'm burning bits of my life. I can see the face of every kid who played those guitars. Funny.' And he threw a bit more of New York on the bonfire.

So, some years later, when the Ratman issued the invite to the Weekend of Wonders, we decided to go. One wet Saturday Leon, my new GPS and I took off to meet up with another mate, Neal. The GPS was courtesy of Sarah; having had enough of me getting lost, she handed it to me as if it were my key to the meaning of life.

Through the rain we drove with the little black meaning of life silent until I needed it. It was only then that it turned out to be the GPS that Burke and Wills would have used; it took us everywhere but in the right direction. The map had the happy knack of disappearing from the screen and a little car would simply float in blue with a large question mark flashing. It did all but spell DIG.

'We've disappeared again,' said Leon and indeed we had, together with the Hume Highway. We found ourselves shuddering along a gravel track.

Leon turned up the volume on the GPS but thanks to Clem it all went pear-shaped. Unknown to me he'd changed the language settings of the little black meaning of life to German.

We prowled around the countryside like a lost Panzer from some bad old war film.

'*Gott in himmel!*' I said. '*Wer ist einer der Veekend of Vonders?*'

'Really sounds like it knows where it's going in German,' Clem said later, by way of explanation.

Then I realised we'd crossed the border and were in New South Wales. Nothing to do with the GPS but with the flashing blue lights of the highway patrol car behind me.

Leon saw him first and told me rather urgently, 'Don't get out of the car, Will, wait for him.'

'It'll be right,' I said.

'Will, don't, he's tiny,' Leon whispered, but I was out of the car by this time.

I looked at the police officer and he looked at me. Up at me. Apart from the guy in the 'Thunderbirds' he was quite possibly the smallest policeman I had ever seen.

'You see those road-work signs?' he said with a voice that sounded like he'd just inhaled from a helium balloon.

'Sorry?' I said.

'The road-work signs informing you to slow down.'

'Oh, err, my GPS.'

'GPS, GPS?'

It sounded like some school chant.

'The language is German. It's speaking German.'

He looked at me. 'You speak German?'

'Only war-movie German,' I admitted.

He stared.

I decided to speak war-movie German. I thought he might like it. '*Jawoll, herr generell. Ze Americana pigdogs. Donner und Blitzen.*'

Not surprisingly, he breathalysed me. When he instructed me to count up to ten into the device, I resisted the temptation to do it in German. Instead, after reaching ten, I explained that the GPS spoke German because my son must have changed it as a joke.

The policeman nodded and sighed. He started writing a ticket, and then sighed even deeper. 'It's not much fun, mate. Scraping people off the road. People. Fathers, sometimes, like you. You probably think I'm an arse giving you a ticket. Just take care, get home and give a rocket to your boy.'

I smiled and nodded. People can often surprise you. The helium copper was no exception.

'Now drive safe.' And then, after a pause, *'Auf wiedersehen, mein Generell.'*

I would have laughed but it took me completely by surprise. He got back into his car and did some paperwork. I thought about him – a highway patrol man, out on the roads, mostly alone – of some of the things he must have seen and how nearly all of the people he came into contact with would treat him in a certain way and how he would treat them. The way he had spoken to me was filled with compassion, and the last deadpan piece of war-film doggerel was simply nonsensical wonder.

When we arrived in Walwa we'd crossed the Murray twice and even through the rain the country was beautiful – valleys with green rolling hills leading up to mountains disappearing into clouds. The valley town looked like a picture postcard, soft and green and lovely, a gentle melancholy suspended over the beauty.

It made me think about the nature of friendship, of how people drift in and out of each other's lives, of how sometimes it seems that a life isn't right without them and yet how suddenly some of those people simply slip away.

Coming into town we passed an old yellow VW Kombi. I saw it from a distance and as soon as I did I thought of Chris. Chris Goethal. He drove a Kombi like the one in front of me, had it for years. The first time I saw him he was parking it at West Footscray Primary School. Climbing out of the car he pretended to pinch a student's bag. The little boy yelled, 'Hey!' and ran after Chris, giggling, and wrested the bag back.

Chris didn't put up much of a fight and kept walking with a smile on his face.

For a while I didn't know what he did at the school, taking him to be a parent, which is exactly what he was. Seeing Chris around the school made you feel safe; it meant there was always someone there to help, to guide and to laugh with. There was Chris Goethal.

Chris not only maintained his enthusiasm through his daughter's and then his son's primary school years, but he also quelled fears that when no more Goethals were students at West Footscray he would drift away like most parents do.

He stayed with us, from the days of securing old boats in the playground, to visits to politicians' offices to badger for extra classrooms and renovations. And from howling with laughter as ropes he'd manufactured from pieces of string snapped as we crossed the Westgate Bridge in a gale force wind, while carrying two prop palm trees back to the Melbourne Theatre Company after we'd borrowed the things to dress up a school carnival. Chris turned to me with a smile as the trees blew, and said in the manner of somebody commenting on the weather in pleasant conversation, 'Oh, William, who would have thought that papier-mâché could be so threateningly exciting?'

There were the hours of meetings on parent committees and school councils and then right on through to the parents' group known as the Connector Bugs, who worked on improving the gardens and environmental surrounds of the school. Some of us have done some of these things – Chris was there through them all, a part of this generation of parents' lives as much as those of the students.

While Sarah was undergoing treatment from her first cancer she stood in line at the local school waiting to vote. Chris – after a day of putting up with sausage sizzles and the orderly propriety of the voting booth – thought he could have some fun with a kindred spirit in Sarah, also sizzling sausages. He sidled up to her and asked, 'Who do you think you are, wearing such an awful hat?' It wasn't until his daughter Rose gave him an almighty elbow in his stomach that he realised something wasn't quite right. He was beyond mortification, because behind his barmy exterior was a man who cared deeply for people.

The next day he appeared with a collection of his favourite songs on a CD, songs that he explained meant a great deal to him. Some of the songs he just liked, some had moved him when he was a little lost and alone. He wanted Sarah to have them. And for her to know he quite liked her hat. It was part gift, part apology and part fun. All Chris.

But the gentleness with which he gave it moved Sarah deeply. Two of the songs ended up on the soundtrack of her film *Look Both Ways*.

He was a funny bloke. In many ways he was a shy man. He never liked being made the centre of attention if people were trying to praise him. But the fact that he found a place in the school community and became part of its bedrock speaks not only of his generosity but also of how much he felt at home there, sensing something in this community that was worthwhile and decent.

At the local supermarket I'd bump into him and have a bit of a chat about nothing and then go on my way to the checkout. I'd empty the basket and a series of objects that I hadn't chosen would be picked up by the cashier, and I would explain I didn't want to buy that large continental cucumber or that jar of Vaseline or those black stockings or that shower cap.

The checkout operator would stare at me and then invariably you'd hear Chris's loud voice somewhere in the queue. 'Do you see what that fellow off the television bought? And now's he's pretending he doesn't want them. Go on, mate, be brave and take the cucumber, you know you want it.'

Some people would laugh, and some would give me a look. There's an old lady who still gives me that odd look when she sees me in the supermarket.

I'd been well and truly Goethal-ed.

One hot summer afternoon I received a phone call from a friend. She was in tears. 'Chris is dead.'

He'd had a massive heart attack.

Why should he be taken so suddenly? Why should a person who worked for so many, die too soon? How would things ever be the same?

Well things wouldn't be the same, but they'd still be. Why try to find a reason? Life can be many things and sometimes it makes no sense. I felt a great imbalance. People like Chris Goethal make the world seem a little safer, a little more generous. And then, as I do invariably when I think about him, I smiled.

Once, on a grade-one excursion to the IMAX theatre to watch a film about giant kelp (that amused Chris no end), Chris and parents including myself were placed at the ends of rows to help any young students to the toilet if the need arose.

It didn't. We looked at a sea of little faces, with funny 3D glasses, arms and hands outstretched, trying to touch the seaweed that wasn't real. They all giggled. Then Chris smiled and giggled with them. He turned to me and said, 'You do have to love the little buggers, don't you?'

And did the children respond? Some years ago, after the afternoon bell had rung, I was kicking a football with a group of students. It included the former school captain Meseret Alem, a young boy who'd come from the Sudan as a refugee. In his short life he'd seen enough of the trouble and rancour that adults, people with ambitions fuelled by intolerance, could bring to a community.

As a ball was bounced end on end Chris walked past, caught it, stuck it under his jumper and waddled around, yelling at us like some demented loon. He dropped the football and threw it back and went on his way.

Meseret looked at him and a smile crept across his face. He said, 'I love that man. Hey, you've got to love that man.'

Chris planted trees around the school that he never saw grow, and in front of the main building are landscaped gardens that he always rabbitted on about. They've grown, blossomed. People at the school thought enough of Chris Goethal to build a monument to him in these gardens. At the side of the path, as it winds around to a little pond that teems with frogs, there's a plaque dedicated to him. There's a rather bemused-looking photo of Chris Goethal on it, as if he's slightly embarrassed by all the fuss. He needn't worry; the garden has grown over the photo, covering it up. He'd be happy with that.

We passed the yellow Kombi on our way to WOW. The driver and passenger got out. A couple of young women. They were laughing about something. I thought of that photo beneath the plants. I smiled.

They looked happy. And I smiled a bit more.

Just after passing the Kombi, we caught up with Neal, wandering along the street holding his finger up like a cricket umpire. I hadn't seen him for a year and his first words to me were, 'You should smell my finger.'

He explained that he had been using the public phone to call us because there was no network reception, but the phone wouldn't work, so he'd tried to get his coin back. 'It was chock full of snails. Somebody's stuffed them in there as a welcome present or it's just the local snail hang-out. I don't know. But you should smell my finger.'

It became one of the catchphrases of the weekend, a non sequitur randomly delivered.

'You don't see many public phones any more, do you?' said Leon.

'Well, you don't see many stuffed with snails, that's for sure,' I said.

'You should smell my finger.'

We made our way to the pub and I wondered what it is about old friends. The three of us had met in drama school and I did a quick sum and realised that I have known them for over twenty-five years. The ease with which we crapped on was testimony to the power of friendship to distort the passage of time. It was as if we had never left each other's company.

The last time we'd been all together was a year before on the beaches of the Mornington Peninsula laughing. We were lolling about on the sand, Sarah and I, Leon and Neal, watching Stella and Neal's daughter muck around in the water. It was a beautiful day and quite still. Leon lay back and said to nobody in particular, 'It's hard to believe that there's a winter, down here on a day like this.'

There were a few hums in agreement and a bit of silence and then Neal said slowly, 'It's hard to believe that I was a Jehovah's Witness on a day like this.'

Leon and I laughed. And then Sarah, who has always had a keener sense of tone, asked him quietly, 'Were you?'

Neal nodded. 'Oh yes. For a year.'

'Why?' asked Leon.

Neal deadpanned, 'I have no idea. Maybe it was a gap year?'

I looked at him. He smiled at me and laughed. 'Don't give me that look, Will,' he said. 'There are lots of lonely people out there, people who just don't talk to many people. And there's a reason for that – they are completely mental.' He laughed and went on, 'I don't think my heart was really ever into it. I mean, there was this elder who was always on my case about not having Witnessed enough.'

'You had a quota?' I asked.

'Oh yeah, "Your numbers are down, Neal! You need to Witness",' he said, putting on a would-be elder's voice.

'You got into trouble?' asked Leon.

'Mate, I was a Witness from the wild side. They were never sure about me. Luckily, there was this old lady who I could go and see, who was always up for a chat. She was a legendary conspiracy theorist. Had a conspiracy for every day of the week. Aliens – Paul Keating was an alien or something. If he wasn't an alien he was an accountant, which is probably the same thing. One on Kennedy – the Masons killed him. She'd be all over the place, always good for a Witness.' He paused for a bit. 'But you know, she was just somebody who never went out.'

'I wonder why?' said Leon.

Neal laughed. 'Exactly. But there's a lot of lonely people and they don't even know they're lonely, it's just life. Sort of sad.'

'Why did you leave?' asked Sarah.

'Sex. Or lack of it,' said Neal. 'I used to Witness with a lovely looking girl. She was about my age. Melissa Titdz.'

We laughed.

'We were just two young Witnesses out there in a car. Feeling horny. We never really did anything, we had no idea.'

'What did you do?' I asked.

'Oh well, we'd Witness a bit and then we'd get all hot and bothered and go into a room and take our clothes off and writhe about on the floor.'

'And that was all you did?'

Neal nodded. 'Yeah, that was enough. We'd lie in the dark and thrash about without touching each other. And then one day Sister Gwen came in looking for her tablets –'

'Sister Gwen?' I said.

'Yeah, Sister Gwen. She was another Witness, an older lady who was on kidney dialysis. She came looking for some tablets and switched on the light and she found us on the floor doing Irish dancing side by side. Bit of rug Riverdance.'

'What did she say?' asked Sarah.

'What did she say …' Neal repeated thoughtfully, then, 'She said, "Where is your pubic hair?"'

We all burst out laughing, including Neal.

He explained he felt so guilty about what he was doing that he thought if he shaved his pubic hair he'd be too embarrassed to do the rug Riverdance.

I said, 'So it didn't work?'

'Obviously not. Mate, when you're on your own – I had no embarrassment whatsoever when the birds and the bees called. Anyway, it was in the dark. Shaven. Bald as Kojak. A real trendsetter.'

His days as a Witness were numbered. He had to front a panel of elders, who interviewed him about what he had done.

'You lay in the dark.'

Neal said he had.

'You took your clothes off.'

Neal said he had.

'You were both naked.'

Neal said they were, but it was dark.

'And you, you, you …'

Neal strained to listen. The elder spoke very quietly and then built in volume with each 'you' that was uttered.

'You, you …' continued the elder before finally asking, 'You plucked out your *pubic hair area*?'

'I shaved my pubic hair area,' said Neal.

It sounded like the scene from *When Harry Met Sally* where she fakes an orgasm in a cafe.

That was it for Neal.

'I got in my car and went and saw poor Melissa and told her I was out and all the rug Riverdancing was over. Said sorry.'

He caught the next bus to Sydney and it was, he assured us, the itchiest bus trip known to man.

We convulsed with laughter on a beautiful beach on a summer's day. The girls in the water, hearing our laughter, looked towards us.

'Don't worry, girls,' said Neal. 'I'm just telling stories.'

What can I say? Life is a smorgasbord, so many dishes to choose from and sometimes you just choose the wrong one, but you know nothing's ever wasted.

We three found ourselves in the pub, as the festival got under way.

It was a real country pub — we're talking Banjo Paterson country pub — and it was here that the arts festival began. Or the Arse Festival, as one farmer called it.

'Here for the Arse Festival, matey?' he asked with a deadpan tone.

I ordered a beer in a suitably manly drawl. Some people sang. A folk band thumped away and other people simply chatted. It was a community of people engaging with each other. And it was fun. That night I heard about the royal engagement for the first time.

'Well, what do you think, Willy?' said a farmer with a face made of leather and hands that had seen more hard work than I'd had hot dinners.

I shrugged my shoulders.

He looked at me. 'Come on, Willy, remember you voting for the Republic?'

'Sure, but I'm in no hurry. Whatever we all want.'

'You'd be moderate!' He laughed.

'What do you think?' I asked.

'Well, he's learnt from his dad and moved on from blondes,' said the farmer. 'Nothing wrong with blondes, of course, but they're more a young bloke's fancy.'

Oh yes.

He nodded. 'Got an old head on his shoulders.'

'Well, he is bald,' I said.

The farmer stared at me. 'True.'

'She's a commoner,' said Lenore the barmaid, whose mixture of homemade and professional tats lent a taste of suburbia to the sticks. For a moment I had no idea what she was talking about.

'Kate. Kate thingy. William's girl. She's a commoner.'

The farmer flicked his paper. 'Says she's middle class.' He smiled a little. 'Now you'd be middle class, Willy?'

'I think she may be a different sort of middle class.'

'More of your upstream middle class? Middle class with a capital M and C?' He laughed.

'Well, good on 'em,' said Lenore.

'Remember his parents' wedding?' I asked.

'Oh Diana, yeah. Had a party as we watched it.'

'Remember she stuffed up his name. No wonder it never worked,' said the farmer.

1981. It had been a soap opera for years: Who will Prince Charles marry?

Lenore poured a beer, laughed and said, 'Prince Charles.'

We looked at her.

'Used to think he was a bit of all right.'

'Yes?'

'He was always out doing things – jumping out of planes, sailing ships.' She shook her head and she laughed again. 'Well, good on 'im. He proposed to her in Kenya. Romantic.'

'Kenya? Well I proposed in the car park of the pub. A number of times.' The farmer winked and downed his beer.

Later, bundled into a minibus, we went to the local winery for the festival's midnight karaoke and there we sang 'Rubber Bullets'. Over and over. It was the only song that came on for an hour – not that anybody seemed to mind.

The winery was a big tin shed and we sat in plastic folding chairs at the entrance. They felt familiar and I remembered a place where I'd sat on chairs very much like these. They were simple to open when you knew how, a bit of a mystery at first but once you got the knack it was all pretty easy – just like a marriage.

That's what Jackie's mum had said at the Footscray Swimming Club; they had the same chairs as the winery.

There are many ways to spend Sunday morning in Melbourne. Sleep in. Go to the galleries. Sit in your favourite coffee shop and do whatever you do in your favourite coffee shop. Or you can spend it with the Footscray Swimming Club. You walk past the woman with the water-aerobics class who likes her music loud. Maybe the people in her class like it loud. Hopefully all the people in the pool complex like it loud, because it's echoing around the Maribyrnong Aquatic Centre.

Across, in the big spa and glass-walled steam room, people sit surrounded by bubbles and wispy jets of smoke. Clem told me once these people looked like dim sims, both steamed and fried. The image has never left me.

You walk on to the end of the pool to the big glass windows with a view stretching down the Maribyrnong River to the city of Melbourne. Here, families mill about on shallow concrete bleachers. Children giggle or sit with friends or cuddle under the wings of parents. It's not a huge club and I suppose it's not unlike many other swimming and sporting clubs across the city, but it represents something, the best of our community. Something special.

The particular quality of Footscray Swimming Club is the make-up of its members. Some seem to have been members since Adam was a lad. In tiny clubrooms are photos from years before, black-and-white images of swimming galas in the thirties and high divers arcing gracefully through the air above the waters of the Maribyrnong. You can see Gordon, barrel-chested and smiling with his arms folded and his hair Brylcreemed to within an inch of its life in a team photo from the fifties and still see him marching along the pool deck every Sunday, organising and smiling and encouraging. Guiding sisters like Jackie and the Sherbet-and-Daryl Braithwaite fan, Caroline; encouraging kids from a seeming rainbow of multicultural backgrounds. Some were born in faraway lands, some are first-generation Australians and others are descendants of members of the First Fleet. They come swimming every Sunday.

I remember one kid in particular on his first day at the club. The little boy stood on the edge of the pool, shaking with the apprehension that everyone feels as they peer into the deep end. But he needn't have worried; Jackie came up and said a few words to him while another parent with a stopwatch gave him a thumbs-up. The little boy was still nervous but didn't feel as alone as he'd felt before. Everybody shouted encouragement and as he splashed along, two older kids were keeping watch and stroking with him. Amazingly, as he finished he beat them. A huge smile stretched across his face and he was cradled in the arms of a sporting club that shows us all a great deal about acceptance, tolerance and community friendship.

Every December the club would organise a Christmas party in the clubrooms, which was about as glorious a secular celebration as you could find.

I was volunteered by Sarah and Jackie into being Santa in a most unconvincing costume and would wander into the first-aid room and stuff a very ordinary Santa-suit full of pillows and first-aid blankets.

It was always made clear to the younger children, who might well have some doubts as to my authenticity, that I was in fact Santa's Australian cousin Neil from Altona, who was standing in for Santa.

Remarkably, one year a little girl asked me what she should call me. Before I could say anything, Jackie said with a smile, 'You can call him Santa Claus because that's his second name, but if you don't want to get too familiar just call him Neilly Santa. That's his full name.'

So that's what the kids called me for a while.

Afterwards, there would be games that I had thought only belonged on old newsreels or in documentaries, such as egg-and-spoon races. Various families would bring dishes, some carefully prepared and some dragged from a cupboard. But everyone always brought something.

It was as if you were among friends, only you didn't really know their names or where they lived or anything much about them. They were just a bunch of families in a little swimming club, whose kids enjoyed swimming up and down the lanes for a while.

But time has a way of catching up with little groups of families.

The club had to share the pool with another racing team. They had a sharp, full-time coach who, like so many swimming coaches, yelled loud and hard and was more interested in results than whether a child can finish a lap with a smile on their face.

The last Christmas I played Santa's cousin from Altona, the little boy who'd been so frightened on the blocks all those years ago had grown up to be a very good swimmer. The coach from the other team that Footscray shared the pool with wanted him to go and train with her. She was apparently a very good coach.

I gave him his present and wished him a merry Christmas and all the other guff we'd carry on with.

He looked at me and said, 'Thanks for this.'

'Oh, I didn't have much to do with it.'

He shrugged and said, 'Thanks anyway. It's my last year.'

'You giving up swimming?'

He shook his head. 'Going over to join Maribyrnong.'

I said that was a shame.

'She's a good coach. And they don't …' He looked around the chaotic room full of people singing and acting up. 'And she's a good coach.' He went quiet.

'You'll be right,' I said and I gave him the thumbs-up.

He looked at me for a moment. 'The first time I swam here you did that, gave me the thumbs-up. The two thumbs-up. Thanks for that.'

I told him it couldn't have been me, because I was Santa.

He smiled. 'Yeah, from Altona.' And he walked back to his family.

People grow and change. And now the swimming club is just a memory, but a good one – those Sunday morning friends, the fumbling with the stopwatches, the echoing music and the kids' laughter – all good.

Life is indeed a smorgasbord with so much on offer. We'll all have our time in the sun. Fashions fade and so does a life, but friendship, between old friends and new, is a tacit agreement between us that we don't have to fade alone.

Realising that is a weekend of wonders. So load up with rubber bullets.

The Lone Ranger
and Tonto
William

Taking Clem to the ballet was me showing Sarah that it was fifty–fifty, that we were partners in being parents, a team and all that entailed. We were the Lone Ranger and Tonto, although who was supposed to be who in the relationship was an open matter. We'd been together as a couple, I suppose, since 1989, and had gone from being a summer fling to being together in a roundabout sort of a way to making a commitment to each other.

How we reached the commitment point happened in part, I think, because we were both too lazy to go anywhere else and also because ever since I opened the front door to a share house in which I was living in Bronte in 1989 and found Sarah standing there, I knew in that same roundabout way that I wasn't *meant* to go anywhere else.

She'd driven up from the south coast to Sydney to catch up with a housemate of mine who wasn't in and so we struck up an argument in the timeless manner of future happily married couples.

It was about beer. We were both heading off to separate parties and Sarah was offering to pick up something from the bottle-o and she didn't like my suggestion of buying a particular type of beer.

'They don't look after their workers and they don't pay proper rates.'

I told her I appreciated this point but that I'd still like that particular drop of beer.

She set off to the bottle-o and returned with a six-pack of XXXX and said, 'This is what you drink if you want to call yourself a Queenslander, not that other stuff.'

I passed on this story rather sulkily to Gordon Fitch, another of my housemates, who looked at me as if I were a fool. 'Mate, you'd do well to hold on to her.'

'What do you mean?'

'She's saved your soul, turned you from the darkness. A Queensland boofhead not drinking XXXX is like me not liking pineapple lumps or L&P, for God's sake.'

'What are pineapple lumps and L&P?'

'Liking pineapple lumps is a mandatory requirement for being a New Zealander. L&P is the legendary Lemon and Paeroa lolly water: New Zealand's gift to the world.'

Gordon, needless to say, was from New Zealand.

So, harbouring a slight niggle for not getting that other six-pack, I followed Gordon's advice and held on to Sarah and she very kindly held on to me.

It wasn't supposed to be that serious a thing and I did my best to reinforce the doubts of me being a long-term prospect with my lack of any real financial holdings, save for a borrowed futon and a poker machine I had discovered on a hard-rubbish weekend along Bondi Road. And an almost total disregard for anything but myself.

Even there, my ownership of the poker machine – a five-cent, crank-handle job – was called into question by Gordon, who claimed salvage rights when he came to help me carry the thing back to the Bronte house.

But it was when we drove in Sarah's battered, push-button S-series Valiant and she put on a Dean Martin tape, which I sang along to word perfectly, that she thought perhaps it might be something more than just a fling.

As I started singing the next song, she gave me a look, waited for me to stop and then said, 'The fact that you know all the words to one Dean Martin song is interesting. The fact you know the words to two is slightly unnerving, but sort of fun.'

And she smiled. And that was that. Sort of. Sarah has that inbuilt fairness gene that demands that things be shared, and not just good things like a box of chocolates or prawns – at dinner once she asked if I wanted the last prawn and I gleefully shrieked,

'Idiot!' as I snaffled the last chilli king prawn and gobbled it down. It was a sad combination of being the youngest in a large family of people who liked their food and being a Queenslander.

She also shared things like responsibilities. When we spoke about this over dinner I nodded and said, 'Sure,' not really thinking that much about anything – it was, after all, the dinner with the chilli prawns.

I took it to be a little bit like organising the car. Oh no – not the kayaks!

But she meant sharing decisions about stuff like where we live, about finances, looking after the kids if we were to go down that path, being around to be a real part of their lives. All that as well as organising the car. And the kayaks. It was about sharing a life together.

I nodded. Then she asked me if I would like the last prawn – I'd been staring at it as she was speaking – and that's when I yelled, 'Idiot!'

Taking on responsibilities or sharing them is something most men probably don't come to readily. Well, most men like me, who haven't had to think beyond themselves and share their life with another person. A man who thinks sharing a life is buying kayaks rather than washing up or managing a house or making sure that bills are paid on time. The kayak syndrome.

And it's safe to say that I was a pretty accurate description of that sort of man; a broke actor and half-owner of a poker machine, who was sleeping on a borrowed futon.

But when you begin to share a life, no matter how awry it goes on occasions, it's the beginning of something splendid.

My father once said that it was fun to be alone and a lad. Running amok, he said, was a fine thing to do. 'But it's when you share a life and you give a part of yourself to somebody else that the fun begins. It's like splitting the atom – bloody smashing, sunshine. It's bloody smashing.'

I don't think anyone really understands that idea until you do give up a part of yourself to another person or people. It's not even about having children or a family or even having a long-term relationship. It is simply about sharing yourself with people. Clem's football coach understood this.

He was a charming, funny and modest man who loved his football and cared for the kids he coached. Once, on the sidelines of a game, he walked back from a quarter-time huddle, grimacing.

'How'd it go, Joe? Fire them up?' said another father.

The coach winced and smiled sheepishly. 'Not much of a homily, I'm afraid. Just told them to go out and enjoy themselves and kick it to the shit.'

'You sound like a parish priest I had once.'

The coach laughed slightly.

I looked at him. That's what he was going to be. Clem had told me his coach was joining the seminary. I thought for a bit and asked him the question before the game took us away. 'What made you want to go and become a priest?' I blurted.

He held his whiteboard with the players' names written on it and I saw my son's. He smiled a little. 'Oh, well. Oh, well …' He smiled again. 'I just love Jesus Christ and his generosity. His love of all of us. I just think there's some good I could do.' He shrugged his shoulders. 'There's lots of people I think I can help.' He looked straight at me.

I nodded. 'Good for you,' I said.

He smiled again and then yelled, 'Oh, come on, kick the bloody thing!'

I thought that there were worse things you could do with a life than be a good person of faith.

But sharing a life and sharing responsibilities, divvying them up between the Lone Ranger and Tonto, if you like, isn't always smooth. If you were being polite, you'd say you have 'discussions', if you were calling a spade a spade you'd say you argue.

I can't remember Tonto and the Lone Ranger arguing, ever. Tonto just spoke in broken English, nodded a lot, held a horse and looked solemn, while the Lone Ranger wore tight trousers, a black mask, stared off into the distance and did all the talking. I don't think the Lone Ranger would have offered Tonto the last chilli prawn and Tonto would only have cried 'Idiot!' under his breath.

Sarah and I, however, argued. Not that much, no more than any other couple – outside the Lone Ranger and Tonto, of course – but the thing that made these arguments special was the fact that we would argue everywhere. In cable cars, on red carpets, in shopping centres, in customs queues, on the way to vote. Almost anywhere.

Once, we had a stand-up shouting match on a lovely spring day on a street corner in Darlinghurst. About what, I can't quite remember, but it was a beauty. I argued and mmm–ed a lot, while Sarah did most of the rational thinking, and talking.

I have always found this an amazingly attractive characteristic of Sarah's – her increased articulateness in accordance with her rising anger, where I relied upon the time-honoured boofhead's tactics. What I lacked in the way of logical debate I made up with in volume. I yelled, but without much effect, just specialising in elongated vowel sounds. And I borrowed from the Lone Ranger's arsenal: the look off into the distance. But here I made the lethal mistake for anyone engaged in an argument: the addition of a slow shaking of my head as I looked off into the distance.

To any sensible person this is like a red rag to a bull. I once saw an eminent and well-regarded ex-senior federal cabinet minister doing almost the very same thing outside a cinema around the corner from where we live, although this poor chump added a parliamentary flourish of outstretched arms to his head shake.

'What are you doing?' he said across the street to a woman who could only have been his wife.

This was a man who had helped alter the course of the nation's history, copping a right royal broadside. She brought all guns to bear. 'Don't you shake your silly head at me! You're not in parliament now. You're just a silly man in bad trousers.'

His reaction was one I knew. He opened his mouth in the manner of a codfish landed on a jetty and let his hands drop to his sides.

And he did have bad trousers.

Sarah let me have it, too; she took my head shaking in and yelled at me, 'Say something! Don't shake your head, you great pompous overblown turd!'

I burst out laughing. 'This is sort of fun,' I said, 'arguing in the street.'

If I wasn't in love before, I was now.

I'm not sure whether Sarah felt the same way, but she did smile after a while.

Not that arguing is always fun but it is a part of being with somebody, or maybe that's just how I was brought up. I remember my father and mother having a shouting match and Dad storming out into the backyard with my mum's voice still cracking hard at his heels. After a few moments of listening to the noise he laughed and said, 'You've got to love a woman with character. And that's the character I love.'

My mother roared again and my father purred, 'Oh, magic.'

I have never failed to feel that slight soaring sensation when I think back to opening the door of that share house in Bronte and finding Sarah standing there, and I never fail to laugh when I remember that argument.

Our relationship reached the point where one morning I felt confident enough that she might accept my proposal of marriage. If she could understand that it had been offered.

We woke up for the first time in the house we had renovated and I left what I thought was a humorous and low-key invitation to officially recognise our union by her side of the bed. Amazingly, it all happened over a rather pleasant argument.

I don't know where I found it but somewhere on my travels I had come across a small plastic figurine of Tonto, the Lone Ranger's faithful, non-arguing partner. He was in an eager kneeling position and was shooting a pistol at some bad-doer – or maybe he just wanted the last chilli prawn. 'Prawn is mine, Kemosabe!'

I thought it might be cute to disarm him with a bit of scissor work and then Blu-Tack onto his hand a small sign upon which I had written, 'Will you marry me?'

I placed the now romantically kneeling Tonto by Sarah's side of the bed. On a small table littered with all manner of stuff.

I waited for a while for a response and I waited a bit more. I waited quite a bit.

Sarah got up and made herself a cup of tea.

I followed her and stared at her. She smiled. I half smiled and she went back to her tea-making. I stared, then she looked up, saw me looking at her and said, 'What?'

'What do you mean?' I said.

'What? That's what I mean. What? What do you want?'

'Is that all you're going to say?' I asked.

She was nearly going to throw the cup at me when I yelled, 'Did you see Tonto? Did you see what he had in his hand?'

Somewhere in the back of my mind something told me that the Tonto proposal might have been a tad too cute.

'What are you talking about?'

'Tonto and his sign. By your side of the bed.'

'There are lots of things by my side of the bed,' she said.

Yes, there were. Perhaps she hadn't seen Tonto. So I led her back to the bedroom and sat her down and pointed to the little green-suited Indian, kneeling. With his sign.

'Oh,' said Sarah.

'So?' I said.

'Well. Does this mean I'm the Lone Ranger?'

'No. No, it just means I'm asking you to marry me.'

'But if you're Tonto, then that makes me the Lone Ranger.'

I hadn't thought about this. They didn't have any Lone Ranger figurines. I thought about it a bit more.

If you want to be the Lone Ranger, then fine, I thought for a moment. The Lone Ranger did all the talking. All the doing. Tonto just sort of hung around.

'Well, maybe I can be the Lone Ranger sometimes?' I suggested.

'What if I don't want to be Tonto? I might like to wear the mask sometimes, you know.'

The more I thought about it the more I thought that I would like to be the Lone Ranger occasionally. I mean, it was going to be fifty–fifty.

'It's important that I'm the Lone Ranger.'

Sarah started laughing.

Right, perhaps I had taken the figurine metaphor a little too far.

She held my hand and looked into my eyes.

This is it, I thought.

'You know there's always been something really gay about the Lone Ranger.'

'And Tonto?'

'No, just the Lone Ranger. He's a bit of an icon.'

'Well, Tonto proposed.'

'You want to be the Lone Ranger.'

'No.'

'Yes, you did.'

'Only sometimes.'

'You want it both ways.'

I swore and stood up. 'Look, would you like to marry me? Can we get married?'

Then I got down on one knee and said the same thing.

She smiled again and said yes. 'Now let's go and have a cup of tea.'

As we walked out she gave me a kiss and said, 'Hi–ho, Silver!'

Interestingly, when we finally *did* get married, it was on the day after we had originally booked the celebrant – a vast, pleasant woman called Mrs Deeath – and organised a room and whatnot down at the old Ozone Hotel in Queenscliff. The reason why there was a day's delay was, of course, on account of an argument. And I can't remember what it was over.

Hi-ho, Silver! indeed.

It was supposed to be fifty–fifty, but things never go that way. I was away from home quite a lot pretending to be other people. Mainly trendy police officers in country towns where a murder took place every fifteen minutes. I would be covered in fake tan, doused with hair dye and parade up and down windy beaches.

But I tried to make up for it in other ways. Before we had Clem we had Doug. Doug the dog, a black kelpie crossed with just enough Labrador to ensure that he wasn't totally hyperactive and who was blessed with the deadpanest deadpan expression I have ever seen.

A short while after Cosmo's death Sarah came home with a little bundle in a blanket; he was apparently the runt of the litter and was being given away by the shop.

We gave Doug a lot of attention and affection and in a way he was one of the great gifts in our lives; after Cosmo died we were fortunate enough to have a wonderful outlet for emotion beside ourselves in the form of dear old Doug.

The great thing about him was that even though he could have been as spoilt as a brat and become one of those weird hybrid beings, Doug never let us forget he was just a dog. He'd look at me with the deadpan Doug special eyes and I knew: 'Don't pamper, just throw the tennis ball,' he seemed to be saying.

And that was about Doug's limit. He'd stare at me and I would throw whatever it was he had brought me – usually a tennis ball, sometimes a stick and sometimes things so bizarre they couldn't fairly be classified as 'fetch' items.

This was a part of my fifty–fifty duties, throwing things for Doug. I spent nearly an hour one night quite happily lobbing a sodden sandwich for him to fetch. It wasn't until my driver's licence fell out that I realised I'd been throwing my wallet for Doug to run after, chase, chew and retrieve. I spent the next hour with a torch, swearing at nothing in particular, while trying to find the contents of the wallet, all the while stalked by Doug, who dropped a slipper at my feet occasionally in the vain hope of another game of fetch.

A different time it was the television remote that he dropped at my feet. I went to pick it up and he grabbed it and looked at me with the deadpan Doug special. I yelled at him and he dropped it and snatched it up again. Then he ran down the hall and I followed, yelling. He dropped it and I lunged as he snatched it, barking.

He ran, I followed. I swore, he barked. Sarah tried to say something and I yelled.

I finally grabbed the remote from him – out in the street, about five houses down from our house. A man I knew beeped the horn of his car as he drove by. 'Looking good, Will!'

I stood, heaving, in a rather unflattering but thankfully fully functional pair of bright green underpants. They were all that stood between me and an indecent exposure charge. Doug stared up at me without the slightest expression on his face. And barked.

I decided that with the impending arrival of Clem I had to take more control over Doug, so I decided to attend dog obedience classes down by the river near Essendon. What made me think I could do anything with Doug I don't know, seeing as I was

barely trained myself, but off I set every Sunday to the classes in what was truly one of the most bizarre periods of my life.

Sarah looked at me and said, 'Are you sure you want to do that?'

'Yes, Doug has to settle down.'

Doug raised his head from where he'd been lying flat out by the fire, wagged his tail a little and gave a friendly bark. And then went back to sleep.

'I just think that dog obedience people are a certain kind of …' Sarah paused, looking for a diplomatic description, 'person.'

'What do you mean?' I asked.

'Oh well, you'll find out.'

Within about fifteen minutes of arriving at a pretty oval by the river I found out. I stood there as an old man was introduced to us as a legend of dog obedience and guidance by a woman with a very energetic manner – like somebody selling an exercise machine on late-night infotainment television.

Here was a man who knew dogs backwards and a man who showed me the way to understand what it is to give a command, to take control: an old man dressed in grey trousers, green jumper, cloth cap and with bandy legs who hobbled around in front of us.

He looked us up and down and then growled at us. Growled like a dog. Then he barked like a dog.

Nobody said anything. I looked at our assembled tribe of dogs and masters; there were animals – and humans – of all shapes and sizes.

The old man stopped growling. Then a fat man with a beagle burped. Very loudly.

The old man growled at him.

The fat man said in a strangled voice, 'Beg yours.'

The old man slapped his thigh. 'Say it as you think your dog would understand it.'

The fat man stood there. We all looked at him.

'Beg yours …' he said slowly.

The old man pointed in exasperation. 'As your dog would understand it!'

The fat man licked his lips and opened his mouth. 'Woof!'

The old man nodded and growled at us.

I looked down to Doug, who stared me in the eye with a deadpan special, as if he were saying, 'Don't you dare, I'm a dog – just throw the ball.'

Maybe the old bloke was just having fun? I don't know. It never really got any better. Mainly because Deadpan Doug had, on occasions, the endearing habit of trying to hump anything that took his fancy. Not all the time, but there were certain attractions he couldn't seem to resist. I worked this out when I was dancing to an old Elvis tune – 'Surrender', I think it was – at a barbecue. I did a pretty ordinary tribute to the great man by striking a Las Vegas karate pose. Maybe it was because I wasn't wearing a sequinned jumpsuit, but I don't think Doug would have cared. A bent knee, it seemed, was his biggest turn-on.

He dropped his tennis ball, attached himself to my leg and thrust away.

I tried to push him off, but he had a Tarzan's grip on my thigh with his front legs and kept going as I lurched around to 'Surrender'.

This party trick was on my mind when the old man asked for a dog volunteer. He wobbled around on his wonky legs and decided on Doug. He took Deadpan, led him to a puddle of water and told him to sit.

Doug did and stayed sitting.

The old man slapped his thigh. 'This is a good dog.'

I was very proud of Doug.

And then he saw the old man's bent knees. Surrender.

Doug applied Tarzan's grip and went to town on the grey trousers. The old man tried to push him down, but I could have told him he had no chance. Then he started to growl.

Doug in deadpan-rutting mode looked up at him without missing a thrust.

The old man growled and Doug seemed to go quicker.

The old man looked to me and said, 'Speak to your dog!'

'Doug!' I yelled.

'As your dog would understand it!' the old man said and growled again.

So there we stood, out on the oval; a growling old man wobbling about while a kelpie humped him with an eternally expressionless face and me toddling around after them yelling, 'Woof!'

Eventually I was given a certificate of graduation for Doug; he achieved a distinction for graduating from Puppy Class, simply because he was too old to go back.

I returned home to Sarah after the first class, but didn't say much and took Doug out to the backyard and threw a tennis ball for him. He seemed to be as old as Moses but he never gave us anything other than deadpan love.

But as he got older he seemed to start shutting down. He'd get caught in corners and half bark in a hoarse, old-man tone and then let off farts. I'd laugh a bit. Sarah would gently lead him back and pat him. 'It's not that funny. He's growing old. Don't laugh too much.'

And she would hold him, this smelly old dog of ours, granting him the dignity he deserved.

When we were renovating the house for about the sixty-fourth time, I wandered over the newly laid kitchen floor – Doug would have been seventeen by this time and his eyes were going, so his tendency to bump into things increased. I heard a bump and looked up to see him walk into a cupboard. I gave him a pat and looked away to inspect the floor and then I heard another sound and a bigger thump.

And there he lay. He tried to get up once and fell down again. I called Sarah at work and she told me to take him to the vet and if it went badly, to give him a cuddle from her and the kids.

He'd had a stroke, the vet said, and really the best thing we could do was euthanase him.

I nodded. The vet left the room and I held Doug. Our doggie dog. Our beautiful deadpan boyo. He was warm and he smelled like the old dog he was. I held him close and felt that awful jittery flight in my chest.

I held him as he was given the needle. I held him as he died. And as I held him I said, over and over, how much we loved him.

I went home and told the builders what had happened and burst into tears. And they downed tools and gave me a cuddle.

'He was a good old dog, that Doug. You just have a cry, mate.'

I couldn't tell Clem or Stella. Sarah said that she would, as I'd gone to the vet's. She was unsure of how to go about it until Clem asked in an absent sort of way where Dougie was. Sarah didn't say anything, just took his hand and looked at him. Then she held him as his face went blank and for those awful few moments that followed, as the understanding of what that loss meant dawned.

Sure, Doug was just an old dog, but he'd been a part of Clem's entire life and a presence in his every day.

He was a sensitive enough boy to know what Sarah was showing him, and I felt a great wave of affection and love for both of them at that instant, witnessing the sharing of something special between a mother and her child.

'I didn't get to say goodbye,' he said quietly.

'I know,' Sarah said, 'I know.'

Life's brief and seventeen years had passed of our lives with Doug in them. Now he was gone. Clem understood passing. There wasn't much to say really. And I could do nothing else except give Stella a cuddle and sit beside Clem as Sarah held him.

I did make some bad fifty–fifty calls with other animals.

Stella came in one afternoon when she was eight or nine and said, excitedly, 'A bunny! A big bunny rabbit is on the street!'

I nodded vaguely and then Sarah laughed from one of the front rooms. 'There is! There's a rabbit!'

We went out to see a morose-looking balloon of white with incredibly long ears. I felt a sinking feeling in my stomach. I knew what was coming next.

'Can we keep it?' said Stella.

'We've got to catch it first,' I said. I turned to Sarah. 'Do we have to catch it?'

'We can't leave it out here, the cats'll get it and it's somebody's pet. They'll be missing it.'

I sighed and we did the good-neighbour thing. Or tried to. For the next hour we chased the rabbit. I had a feeling that it didn't want to be caught. Sarah finally threw a blanket over it.

She picked it up and the animal wriggled about in her arms like an atomic explosion.

We made up signs and posted them around the neighbourhood: *Has anyone lost a rabbit?*

And we gave a description: *Fluffy white large rabbit with long ears.*

We should have added: *Also has foul temper. And is a deranged would-be serial killer.*

Nobody came to collect it, so it stayed with us. It would get out of the makeshift hutch I had constructed and scramble around the yard. Under the house it would go and we would follow. The kids thought it was funny. Until the rabbit – which Stella had christened Mr Snowy – scratched her.

'Mr Snowy' even *sounded* like a serial killer and I wondered what other crimes this freak of nature could get up to.

I took charge. I'll take him to the vet, I decided, and see what we can do.

Sarah laughed. 'What, give him some rabbit-soother drugs?'

'Well, maybe, but Mr Snowy has to calm down!'

'Perhaps there are rabbit obedience classes you can go to?'

I just growled at her.

The vet told me Mr Snowy was a French Lop.

'Yeah?' I said.

'Yeah,' said the vet. 'They are pricks of things.'

I nodded heartily.

'Is there anything you can give him to calm him down?'

'Oh, I suppose anthrax or the calicivirus might be the go.' I looked up at him. 'Sorry, just a bit of rabbit humour there.'

He went into considered vet-thinking mode and came up with something that a talkback radio caller would be proud to own up to: 'I could cut his nuts off. That helps to calm them down.'

I said, 'All right,' and I looked at Mr Snowy. 'Well, you deserve it, old chum.'

Mr Snowy returned home not quite the complete French Lop he had been when he left. He lost his nuts in more ways than one that day, becoming completely insane. He was out for vengeance and he wanted a piece of anyone who came near him. It was like having Joseph Stalin as a pet.

In the end we were captives in our own home, never knowing when Snowy Stalin – that's *Mister* Snowy Stalin – would get out and wreak havoc.

It finished one afternoon when a woman knocked on our door and asked if by any chance we had seen a large white rabbit.

'A French Lop?' I asked, excitedly.

'Yes,' she said.

'We've got him in the backyard.'

'Oh, thank goodness,' she said.

I looked at her and she at me.

'Well, would you like me to get him?' I said.

Perhaps I sounded a little too eager – maybe she thought it was the old 'Yes, I've got your insane French Lop in my backyard' routine. So I girded my loins and fetched the fluffy psychopath. He came surprisingly easily for him, giving me only a few scratches.

I handed him over and the lady was very grateful. She offered me some money for looking after Snowflake, as it turned out he was called – maybe that's why he was so angry at life, perhaps he was rebelling against his name? But I refused. Her taking the thing out of our lives was payment enough.

She held Snowflake and just before she went said, 'We were so worried; he's a special rabbit. We breed and show them, you know, and he's our breeding male. So thank you very much.'

I nodded slowly.

Clem had heard and came to the door as the woman and rabbit got into a waiting car and said innocently, 'But didn't we castra –'

'Shush!' I said. 'Just wave goodbye to Snowflake.'

The woman smiled as she got into the passenger's seat.

She held up the rabbit and – maybe it was for Clem's benefit or maybe it's a rabbit breeder's thing – she waved one of Mr Snowy Stalin's paws.

The look on the nutless rabbit's face stays with me to this day.

Mr Snowy would have livened up the ballet that I took Clem to see. I had a choice of three ballets that would convince Sarah that I was not trying to turn him into a mini super-bloke.

She had pointed out that I often spoke to him in terms of sport and had taken a great deal of pride in his ability to kick and hit balls of various shapes and sizes.

It was when I was proudly displaying my dislocated and warped fingers and floridly telling him which rugby match had caused that particular break and which dropped cricket ball had caused the other that Sarah pointed out I hardly spent any time talking to Clem about art or poetry. Two things I quite like.

As I remember, I sulked a bit and then decided to show how serious I was about rounding out Clem's life education by taking him to see a ballet.

Fifty–fifty? I'll give you fifty–fifty. Ballet. I'll show you I'm not some super-yob. Ballet.

There were three on offer: *The Nutcracker*, *Swan Lake* and *Spartacus*.

I chose *Spartacus*. Why? Well, because I am a super-yob. Couldn't have *Swan Lake* or *The Nutcracker*, bit too … Well, poncy. No, go for *Spartacus*; a manly ballet about Kirk Douglas and slaves and gladiators. And it had music from 'The Onedin Line'; manly music from a manly television series about boats.

All this I knew because my bloke antenna was quite alert.

So there we sat watching men in baggy leather nappies and GI Joe-type make-believe facial growth pretending to fight and gladiate with wooden swords. They were great dancers but it was because they were gladiators they made great dancers. I did try to shift my point of view, tried to appreciate them as dancers. And I told Clem that we should follow this form of storytelling and expression.

'They walk funny. Like they've done their hammies.'

'Listen, Clem, follow the story! It's a good one about Spartacus.'

'It's that old movie you like.'

I nodded.

'Is that your favourite old movie?'

'No,' I said.

'What's your favourite old movie?'

'Shush,' I said. 'Watch the ballet.'

We watched for a minute and just as I was thinking they *did* walk like they'd done their hamstrings, Clem leant over and said, 'Is *Guns of Navarone* your favourite old movie?'

I said, 'Yes.'

He paused as Spartacus did something very tender to his Roman noblewoman wife. It was a dramatic moment because the music was soft and the dancers were hardly moving. Spartacus was stretching his hamstrings, reaching towards her, and she was fluttering on her toes.

'Is there a ballet of *Guns of Navarone*?' asked Clem.

I laughed a bit. Then a bit more. '*Guns of Navarone*, The Ballet. Very good.'

It was when the Roman general came on in his white cape and with golden laurels around his head that I knew that Clem had missed the ballet bus.

'He looks like Mr Snowy,' he said.

Spartacus versus Mr Snowy Stalin with an homage to *Guns of Navarone* thrown in. Now *that* would have been a ballet worth seeing.

On the way home on the train I tried to tell Clem why I'd taken him to the ballet. 'It's because I wanted you to see other stuff besides footy and cricket.'

'But I like footy and cricket.'

I nodded.

'And soccer, and basketball and fishing.'

'Yes, but there's other stuff out there. Lots of other stuff you may not even know you like.'

'Like ballet.'

'There are heaps of ballets. Just because you didn't like that one, doesn't mean you might not find one you like.'

Clem looked at me. 'It had men in leather nappies, Dad.'

'Well, yes it did. And they were pretty good dancers.'

An old lady looked across at us.

'I liked going with you, Dad, and if you want to go see men in leather nappies then that's okay.'

The woman looked at me. I smiled and she turned away.

We didn't say much more and when we got off at Footscray, before I left the train carriage, I turned round to her and said, 'I'm Spartacus.'

There's nothing like having a go at something people think is impossible, and seeing it work out.

Sending men to the moon was impossible, but they got there. I wasn't aiming for the moon; I was just trying to fix my dunny. It leaked.

I was going to try to take another of the doing-it-fifty–fifty alleys; I was going to go handyman, having first gone the usual route of getting somebody who knew what they were doing. I had called the plumbers, but despite their supposed best intentions they didn't seem interested in stopping a leak.

How hard could it be?

I announced to the family that I'd be mending the toilet.

They stared. I couldn't blame them. My track record as a tool master isn't great. My father never had any illusions. 'If you were putting Christ on the cross, you'd have just nailed yourself up there instead of him. Go to uni.'

And, later, there was the fury of a ragingly insane high-school manual arts teacher. In Brylcreemed and long-socked glory an apocalyptic woodwork teacher we called Donger roared as he inspected my mournful cheeseboard. '*This?* Shameful! This, a cheeseboard? It's a cheeseboard disgrace!'

Who'd have thought a piece of particle board could incite such passion?

Undeterred, I marched to Bunnings.

'A washer should fix it,' said Bunnings man.

I have a blind faith in people with aprons and name-tags. No reason to doubt Bunnings man. He was my aproned Obi-Wan Kenobi. On the evolutionary handyman level he seemed right up there. Problem was, I was Neanderthal handyman. A Cro-Magnon Luke Skywalker.

'Shouldn't take more than a few minutes.'

I came looking for him again after two hours of unsuccessful plumbing work.

Aproned Obi-Wan wouldn't look at me. He felt a great disturbance in the Force and ran for another aisle.

Another Bunnings Jedi – more Samuel L. Jackson than Alec Guinness – stirred me.

'Come on, man! Don't muck around with washers, get a new cistern! Go for it!'

I took home my cistern.

I was happily singing to myself, enjoying the acoustics, when I heard Stella on the cordless phone. 'My dad is trying to fix the toilet. Yes, the toilet,' she said to a friend. 'Your dad is playing golf, my dad has his head in the toilet. Singing.'

Her friend spoke.

My daughter answered. 'It's Dean Martin – I think.'

I nodded.

'Dean Martin,' said Stella. 'He's going through another Dean Martin phase.'

She listened and then said, 'Some singer in a dinner jacket.'

They both laughed.

I will show them, Bunnings man told me.

Another two hours passed and I wanted to flush Bunnings man's head down the toilet.

Except it didn't flush.

But suddenly, somehow, some way, things stuck together. Nothing leaked.

I don't know what Michelangelo did when he finished his Sistine Chapel, but finishing my Cistern Chapel, I was euphorically giddy. Or perhaps it was because the cistern was off-centre, giving the whole toilet experience an off-key, oddly floating look, making going to the loo a bit like riding on the sideshow alley favourite, The Gravitron. But it worked. I said, almost wistfully, 'That's one for you, Donger.'

Sarah came in and had a look as I admired my handiwork. She put an arm around me and said, 'I knew I married you for a reason.'

In a way I blame my mother. In the 1970s there was a television show my parents loved, especially Mum. It was called 'The Good Life' and dealt with a couple who opted out of 'the rat race' (what a seventies concept that was), by becoming self-sufficient in their comfortable suburban home. They had pigs and chooks and veggie gardens and home power all seemingly designed by the Professor from 'Gilligan's Island', and all in their backyard.

As I remember, it was because the husband, called Tom Good, decided he'd had enough of the rat race and his wife tagged along without question. The husband spoke very, very quickly as if he'd had a couple of huge nostrils of cocaine and like he'd been to a party at a 1980s dance club. His wife smirked a lot and said, 'Oh Tom' as if she knew what he'd been up to at the dance club.

The couple had gormless neighbours called Jerry and Margo who wore the weirdest clothes and were supposed to reflect mainstream society. Neither of the couples had children and seemed to belong to some nursing home rather than the suburbs. Maybe that was just England at the time.

Something about this show really struck me – I thought that it would be rather nice to have chickens in the backyard, and my mother encouraged this. While Tom and his wife tut-tutted along with Jerry and Margo, Mum would stare at the telly and say to nobody in particular, 'It'd be nice to have some chooks again.'

My father would say nothing. Sometimes there was a slight shrug of his big shoulders and a quick sideways look to Mum. If she looked back at him he'd mutter, 'Not bloody likely.'

My mum had had some chooks when I was a little boy and was always keen to have more. I liked how the chooks on the TV wandered here and there and always managed to get out of the way if somebody ran about through the Goods' backyard.

In fact chickens were a staple of many minutes of film and telly that I have watched in my life. Cars, trucks or even horse-drawn carts pulled up into whatever make-believe yard was the set of the show and miraculously the chickens would cluck out of harm's way. They were bucolically self-sufficient. Reality, of course, is very different.

Chickens, as I found later, were where the dinosaurs went. I understood my father's sidelong glance and uncomfortable shoulder shrug but you only realise these things when you live through them. Call it a hangover from 'The Good Life', or perhaps I

myself went to one too many dance parties in the eighties, but I decided it would be good to have chickens. Sarah agreed. This was where all the kitchen scraps would go.

We inherited a couple of chooks from a friend who couldn't believe her luck that somebody was stupid enough to want to take them off her hands, and I constructed a chook pen that was next to useless. In it we shoved the first brigade of our chooks. The children gave them names: Chicken Tonight and Henny Penny.

They were allowed to run free in the backyard. Free range. They shat like maniacs and pecked feet at random. I could hardly bear to pick them up and screamed at the kids to try to wrangle them. They laid eggs everywhere but inside the pen that was built for them; occasionally on the trampoline or under the outside lounges, sometimes in forgotten piles of washing. Even more uncomfortable, my cricket kit bag was often a desired nest, which led to a sulfur-scented stay at the crease the following season.

They didn't last long. A builder's dog got Chicken Tonight – that name was tempting fate – and Henny Penny just grew old.

After their demise a year went by and suddenly Stella wanted some pets. Back from Vic Markets came some chooks in a cardboard box. They had been hand-reared according to the man who sold them to us. Hand-reared by Jack the Ripper.

These things were borderline psychotic and were kept in a tin hen house I bought from a shed-maker. It was christened Pent Ridge because of the warmth of its character, but even it didn't seem able to contain its inhabitants, Super Max and Isa Brown. All I can say is that incarceration didn't solve any deep-seated behavioural problems these creatures may have had. They didn't really do anything except eat and shit and attract the odd unfortunate rat into their orbit.

They disappeared in due course and I thankfully had the chooks out of my system.

That is until my mother encouraged my children.

Mum ended up getting a couple of chooks that routinely produced an enviable amount of eggs at a quality that was superior enough to win first prize at the local show. Her chooks were of a rather peculiar pedigree and character. One was called Flopsy because it had an endearing tendency to flop down all of a sudden and cluck happily to itself. The other was quaintly given the name of Boudoir Raider; this was also after a personality trait described by my mother. 'The bastard of a thing gets in the house and lays eggs on the beds.'

It was usual to see my mother, early in the morning, roaring at the top of her voice in pursuit of the chook as it prowled from one bed to another. 'Boudoir, Boudoir come here, you bugger! Oh you're a clever chooky chook, you've given me an eggy!'

My children, especially Stella, were disappointed if Mum and her hens didn't put on a bit of a show. It was always a Nanna Mac thing, and when any of us thought about her it became almost impossible not to draw an image of her and her house and her dogs and her chooks.

It can be funny what you hang onto in grief and when my mother died Stella started asking if she could have some chickens again. I did my best to ignore her but Sarah thought perhaps it might be a good idea; they would be something Stella could care for and look after as well as being a tangible connection to my mother. I shrugged my shoulders and gave my wife a sideways look in honour of Dad, but I could see that what she said made some sort of sense. 'Some' being the operative word.

With Sarah's cancer recurrence, our lives were in a state of flux, especially hers, and maybe the whole idea of happy chooks would give Stella some stability, a chance to have some order over a little part of her life. Sarah also couldn't say no to any proposition that had the potential to make someone happy.

Stella wanted to have a Nanna Mac memorial chook shed, so I set off to Bunnings and came back with a totally impractical but very attractive chook shed that looked more like a doll's house. Stella was very happy. Off to Vic Market with a shoe box, and there was a bored-looking chicken man who picked his nose as Stella carefully chose the chooks that would occupy the Nanna Mac chook shed.

'Mate,' I said as the chicken man excavated his nose some more, 'are they all chickens?'

He looked at me as if I were an idiot.

'Dad,' said Stella, 'what do you think they are – donkeys?'

'No, I just mean, are there any roosters in there?'

He gave a small shrug. 'Just bring them back if they are.'

Here I felt a small shiver of doubt. 'How will I know if they're roosters?'

Now he knew I was an idiot. 'Matey, if they crow they're a rooster.'

We decided to buy five chicks, five because there was a possibility that some mightn't make it through to the big house. This sort of seemed sensible but also slightly insane. Five. That's a lot of chickens. Five fluffy little balls of life following Stella around. Following all of us around.

They were all given names: Russell Crowe, Gregory Peck, Raptor, Cheeky Beaky and Glynnis. Where that came from heaven knows. But they all thrived. For a while. I think it was Glynnis who started looking a bit dodgy one morning, staggering a little here and there and shivering.

Even though the chicks all formed a goodbye gaggle as she left for school, Stella said quietly that she didn't think Glynnis was very well. We assured her that we'd look after her so Sarah wrapped the chick up warmly in an old baby blanket and kept vigil; the last thing we wanted was another death. Even a chook death. I heard Stella thank Sarah and tell her she would look after Glynnis when she came home that afternoon; the fact her mother was undergoing another course of chemotherapy wasn't lost on her and the chook's health became important to us all, even Clem, who up until then had been quite uninterested.

Poor Glynnis didn't last the morning, so Sarah placed her – or whatever it was – back into her shoebox and waited to break the news to Stella. We decided that we should have some sort of service and tell Stella she could choose the music and ask a few people over. This would be good, everything would be fine.

It was a beautiful sunny day and so I decided to hang some washing out and I laughed a little as I stomped about in my giant green Crocs with a plastic washing basket and the four remaining chickens running this way and that as I hung out the clothes.

They were supposed to never get hit, chickens; they always got out of the way on the television. I heard little chirping noises, shushed them away and took a few more steps. And then. The chirps stopped and I knew instantly what I'd done. I felt them through the foam soles of those bloody Crocs. Two little bumps.

I don't know what it was, maybe because the chickens were half tame and were expecting a scrap of food or some form of attention from me. Well, they certainly got that from the green Crocs. I roared in grief at what I'd done. For what I'd lost – my mother. And what I feared losing – my wife. I threw down the plastic washing basket and ran screaming up into the backyard and wailed under a tree.

The two remaining chicks followed me.

I couldn't bear to look and I yelled to Sarah, 'I've just killed the chickens. Did I just kill Russell Crowe?'

Russell was everybody's favourite.

'No,' said Sarah. 'But I don't think Gregory Peck made it.'

'Gregory Peck,' I moaned.

Sarah gave me a cuddle and then went and cleaned up what was left of the chickens.

This I must admit was above and beyond and I decided I too must leap into action. It was a kayak moment. Stella must have more chickens. I looked at the clock and told Sarah, 'I can do this.'

We didn't really need any more chickens.

I looked across at the chook-dolls' house. 'Nanna Mac' was painted upon a sign that hung on the gable.

'I have to get more chickens,' I said, very much in the manner of Harrison Ford.

I think Sarah nearly laughed but managed to give me a pat on the back and I took off.

I grabbed the only box I could see, which was of all things a Dom Perignon champagne box, a present for some unutterably bad acting job I had been associated with.

I raced to the chicken man. Unbelievably, he was picking his nose. He stared at me and nodded. I nodded back. 'You back for more?' he said.

I took a breath and attempted slowly to tell him what it was that I had done. Maybe it was the chooks, maybe it was my daughter, maybe it was my mother and maybe it was my wife. All these things were swirling around in my head. My daughter and her sad little heart, the first understandings of mortality, the loss of my mother. And then I thought of how I made Sarah clean up Gregory Peck. I felt most ashamed about that. It all welled up inside me and this chicken man copped a full side of emotion.

I bawled.

'I killed my daughter's chickens.' And I cried. In front of a Friday afternoon crowd at Vic Markets. 'I was hanging out the washing and I stepped on the chickens. On Gregory Peck and I think, I think it was Raptor.'

Some part of me knew this wasn't a good look. The chicken man stared blankly back and said warmly, 'They're just chickens, mate.'

I cried a bit, then nodded and said, 'Three chickens, please,' and blubbed a bit more.

From nowhere somebody put an arm on my shoulder.

'It's okay,' said a voice and I looked to see what I thought was a woman, a very tall woman, patting me on the shoulder. 'It's okay, it's so good to see someone like you show emotion in public.'

She was wearing a dress, that's why I thought she was a woman, but when I looked at her face I noticed she had a beard. A neat, trimmed beard and very red lips. And a beauty spot. Nevermind, he/she was being very nice. But then he/she looked down at the box I had brought for the chickens as the chicken man skewered it with air holes.

'Oh, you drink Dom Perignon, do you?'

There was a tone in he/she's voice.

'Oh, it was just a present from a job.'

The chicken man looked on and had his hand outstretched. 'Ten dollars for the three, thanks, mate.'

'You live in Footscray and you drink Dom Perignon, do you? You're one of *those* people,' he/she said.

I didn't know what 'one of *those* people' was but I didn't particularly care, I had to get home before Stella.

I ran through the market with my Dom Perignon box full of replacement little fluffy chicks and got in the car and thought I could still reach the backyard in time.

Along Dynon Road and the traffic wasn't too heavy. Yes, I could still make it.

That's when I saw it. It wasn't a little fluffy thing; it had gone past that stage. It was big enough to get out of the Dom box and leap up onto the dash. It was a weird beaky looking pecking animal.

'Holy shit!' I heard myself scream and the creature hopped onto the seat.

The car crossed lanes a couple of times while I screamed like Gene Hackman in *The French Connection* and I remembered the crazy driver in LA. In between my screams I thought for a moment, This thing is slightly bigger than the other chickens.

I looked in the box and saw the other two replacements, they were even bigger.

At home I managed to get the thing back into the Dom Perignon box and ran around the back and tossed them all into the chook yard. Stella was sitting on the back verandah with Sarah.

'I told her,' said Sarah.

'You told her?' I shrieked.

'Mum said there was an incident with a washing basket.'

Sarah smiled wanly. An incident with a washing basket. What a great euphemism for an inexplicable disaster. She should have worked for the Pentagon.

I fell quickly into line. 'Yes, there was an incident with a washing basket, a white plastic washing basket.' I'd added too much information.

Stella looked at the white plastic washing basket, which was now empty.

'A washing basket full of clothes. Wet clothes. Very heavy. Dangerous.'

Stella stared at me and I nodded. I looked at the chickens in the coop. The big ones were pecking the little ones. I stared down at the Dom Perignon box in my hands.

One of *those* people.

It couldn't get any worse, only of course it did.

Months went by and the chickens just became chickens. Their names sort of disappeared. Even Russell Crowe became just another chook, and then it happened. It was the way they jumped on top of the old Wahu rugby ball and flapped their wings and did wanton things to it. Then one by one the bloody birds started to warble in their throats and finally crow.

I tried to tell myself and Stella and Sarah that all chickens did that. But the birds seemed to take some dumb wonder in crowing with all their might, proclaiming their uselessness before the world.

Chooks are one thing, but roosters, well that's a one-way ticket.

We couldn't tell which ones were which. We weren't sure which one was starting to crow, but I thought it was the one with the limp, so Sarah came up with the idea of tying little strands of yellow wool on the legs of the roosters we caught in the act. 'Limpy' was the first, but eventually they all seemed to gather the dreaded banner.

One morning Sarah looked at me and then we both looked at the five roosters that wore the yellow thread and crowed from the pretty little gables of the chook-dolls' house. 'We'll have to get rid of them.'

In an act of desperation I rang the lost dogs' home. 'What can I do about roosters?'

'Do you have a rooster?' came the soft voice.

'Yes, I have five.'

'That's a lot of roosters to have.' There was a pause. 'Are you a chicken fancier?'

'Well, I eat lot of it but I wouldn't call myself a fancier.'

'Are you a breeder?'

'No, I bought them from the markets, they were supposed to be chooks but they turned out to be roosters and now they've all got bits of wool on so I know they're roosters and I think I have to get rid of them.'

'Five is a lot of roosters.'

'Do you get rid of roosters?'

'No.'

'Who can help me?'

The whole conversation sounded like something out of a bad mafia movie.

'I know someone who may be able to help you,' said the soft voice, 'but they don't come cheap.'

'Who?'

'The RSPCA.'

I rang them in search of a chicken hitman and another soft voice spoke to me. I explained my problem.

'We can help you. We can put your chickens to sleep. We can euthanase them.'

'Great!' I said. 'How much will that cost?'

'One hundred and forty dollars per chicken.'

'One forty per rooster?'

'Roosters? Oh roosters are more.'

'How much?'

'One hundred and forty-five.'

'Why the five-dollar difference?'

'I don't make the rules, I don't set the price. I just do the job. And,' there was a pause, 'a rooster is a rooster, not any old chicken.'

I thanked the soft voice and burst out laughing. It was quite insane really and if my mother were around she would have been laughing most of all.

I turned to Sarah and told her the news; she laughed as well and then got that look in her eye. The look of a deeply rational thinker. 'We have to get rid of them.'

By this I took it she meant me.

I shrugged and gave a sideways glance and suddenly understood why my father had never wanted to get any more chooks. So it had come to this.

'We bought them, we should take responsibility for them,' said Sarah, and I knew she was right.

I remember my father trying to kill a chook. Somebody had told him that you grab them by the legs and give a strong flick and quickly break their necks. My father roared his desperation and looked like some crazed cheerleader as he tried to painlessly snap the unfortunate chicken's neck.

'Oh for Christ's sake! Holy Mary,' was all he yelled as he shook.

I wasn't going to go down that track, so I turned to the trusty tool of the modern man, the Internet.

The first method under the googled term of 'humanitarian ways of killing a chicken' was the cheerleading strangle and then some other indecipherable methods including using a broom handle that you place between your legs and then putting the chicken's throat under it and grabbing it by its legs and pulling it through.

I printed this page out as it seemed the cleanest way to go about accepting my responsibility. I got up and wandered around saying, 'We can't kill them. We're not going to kill them, are we?' I got a broom handle, had a few practice golf swings.

I came back about ten minutes later and was going to ask Sarah where the printout was. She was sitting on our back verandah. A broom handle not far from her, the printout at her feet. And a chicken in her lap. She stroked the chook very delicately. It was the one with the limp. She held the thing close to her and said softly, 'There we are.'

I said very helpfully, 'We can't, you're not, are you?'

She looked up at me. 'I've never killed anything before, on purpose.' And the lifeless chook lay there in her arms quite peacefully.

I sat down beside her. 'It's only a chicken, that's what the chicken man said at the markets.'

'Maybe. But it was a life.' Sarah took a deep breath.

For once the Internet had been right. It was over very quickly and the chook didn't make a sound.

'No, I've never killed anything before.' She gave the chook to me.

It was Cheeky Beaky. I remembered its name. I looked at the other roosters. They didn't seem to notice Cheeky's demise.

'I'll take care of the rest,' I said, gallantly, to Sarah.

She nodded her thanks with her best 'as if' expression and we held hands.

'Well, first we should pluck it,' Sarah said gamely.

This really was 'The Good Life' gone Gothic. No wonder that guy who was in it spoke so quickly.

So we sat together on our verandah plucking a chook. Sarah bald and gagging and me just gagging.

'Sorry,' said Sarah, 'I can't do this anymore.' She raced to the toilet.

I carried on a bit longer. The feathers coming out and skin looking a little too white, feeling too warm. I stopped and Sarah called out to me from inside. 'You don't have to go on.'

Cheeky Beaky. I remembered its name. I said it slowly to myself.

'Come inside.'

Stella came home and I told her about Cheeky Beaky. How we had killed her. How Sarah had to kill her. Him. Kill him. So we could eat him. Because we ate chicken.

'But they're pets.'

We both nodded, neither of us mentioning that poor old Cheeky wasn't going to be eaten and neither were the rest of the flock. Well, not by us.

'Which one was that?' said Stella. Quietly.

Sarah started to describe Cheeky, gave up and then said, 'Oh, you know, the one that crowed.'

Stella said, 'We didn't need the chickens to make us think about Nanna Mac. She's always around us somewhere.'

I nodded.

Later that night I drove down to the Arts Centre and deposited four roosters, who happily roosted in a tree there. This was Stella's idea when she saw me wielding a broom handle and studying the printout. She told Sarah that, 'Most artistic people are nice, they might like chooks. Maybe we can leave them at the centre.'

Under cover of darkness I left them there with some food, nesting quite happily in a tree.

I don't know what became of them but in my mind's eye they are happily crowing in some garret with a painter, covered with daubs of paint and chook shit.

The chook-doll's house still sits in the side garden, its Nanna Mac sign hangs from the gables. It's uninhabited and is almost certain to remain that way. But every time I see it there I smile to myself. Worse things, they say, happen at sea.

Cloudy Days

Sarah

I can't be sure when or where my love of the water – watching it, being in it, painting it – began. But I can't imagine it ever being unimportant to me. I love its cycle, moving from rivers and oceans, to clouds then rain, tides linking to the phases of the moon and the moon to the stars. If I can't figure out what everything else in the world is about, I can always be calmed by the simultaneous predictability and unpredictability of water and the weather. Walking along a beach is the most soothing thing I can do.

It isn't as if I grew up near the sea or even by a river. My first years with water were probably limited to a small bath with my sister and being told firmly to never ever leave a tap dripping. We grew up in Cooma in New South Wales, on the high plains at the base of the mountains.

My father was a hydroelectric dam designer – in my teenage years, a job about as popular with my peers as being a baby-seal clubber. In Cooma, he worked on the Snowy Mountains Scheme, believing in clean electricity and running water for all households, something I am sure he never imagined would one day be considered a debatable good.

As small children we would sometimes go on picnics and, like most children, play at his job on a small scale, using stones and sticks to divert creek water and ourselves for the day. We watched valley towns move as the valleys filled with water, treetops still visible on the rises. I learnt to swim in the Murrumbidgee River and at the local pool. I have memories of the river's cold, clear water – the snow-melt – running over rattling stones, the bright aqua pool at odds with the subtle colours of the Monaro district. There are photos of us visiting friends on the south coast and over-excitedly jumping waves in the shallow surf and going to see our grandparents in Sydney, wearing jumpers over our bathers while messing about in a tinnie. But these would be rare occasions. Perhaps having only glimpses of water added to my infatuation with it.

Once, on our way to Sydney, we drove for hours and hours to visit a dam. My father, who saw no reason to stop for toilet breaks or food, thought nothing of a three-hundred-kilometre detour to see a dam wall. Only now do I understand that some dam walls truly are amazing structures – the water high and close on one side, often a sickening drop below on the other.

We walked along the wall and I looked at the water on both sides; the river far below flowing slowly, rippling around moss-covered rocks into tempting pools, the high water on the other side still five metres below us, cool and refreshing but un-swimmable. I felt I could fall down into it; I wanted so much to be a part of it that I started to feel sick. My mother took me back to the car, thinking my wooziness was the vertigo she herself suffered from. She gave me a drink of water and I stopped needing the swim. Maybe my love of water is really courtesy of a tendency towards dehydration.

We moved to Melbourne when the hydro scheme was wrapping up. It was the beginning of the summer holidays. My mother, staring down the barrel of six weeks with three girls and no friends, quickly enrolled us in the first club she saw – the local swimming club.

My adolescence from then on was spent being either in love with the idea of being a swimming champion or with one of the boys in the club. Occasionally both at the same time. But I never got a boyfriend or became a champion. The pool was only open from November until the end of March and any small movement of boy towards girl or vice versa would be cut short by a winter full of self-doubt and comfort-eating, leaving me chubby, shy and overly self-conscious at the start of the new season.

Still, I lived for the pool opening day each spring and the worst punishment my mother could hold over me would be the denial of my season ticket to the pool.

In the water I felt as fast and smooth as a seal or a penguin. I loved it, loved so many things about it. Being weightless, unwatched. I felt graceful as I dived beneath its surface and curved like a dolphin through the deep, before pushing off and leaping out of the water briefly to dive back under to the quiet. I also loved swimming competitions – no talking, no one to witness my fierce competitiveness or giggly laughter, depending on the day. Swimming fast, swimming faster. No 'Who's got the ball?', 'Pass it to me, to me!' or team selection, where I would stand unpicked and, in my mind, unloved. Instead, it would just be me up on the blocks, looking ahead, diving and swimming as fast as I could. Nothing but the black line, aqua water and the patterns and shadows of my movements on the pool floor.

My father, a scholarship boy for both school and uni, valued education very highly, and sacrificed a lot to send my two sisters to a private school for their education and wasted good money on me.

One of the sacrifices was family holidays. We didn't have one until I was almost sixteen, when we drove excitedly to Queensland and a fibro flat four blocks from the sea. Queensland for the first time; it was the beginning of a long love affair. Sunshine, surf, wide beaches, vibrant colours, green mountains and exotic fruit – my first tastes of mangoes and avocados. Sandy pineapple pieces in Tupperware on the beach and fresh bread rolls taken back with sandy feet up the outside stairs, through the squeaking screen door into the flat. Its lino floor, Laminex four-seater table, single lounge and Scrabble set becoming my indelible picture of the perfect beach house.

We swam all day and when we weren't in the water we lay on our towels, toasting ourselves with coconut oil; the squawk of seagulls, other holiday makers' squeals and shouts and the crashing waves blending and fading into a drifty summer dreaming.

We learnt to bodysurf, surely one of the most exhilarating things in the world to do. 'And it's free!' we shouted at each other. After much tumbling, dumping and bathers adjusting my older sister and I swam out beyond the breakers to rest, floating idly, looking back at the swells – temporarily hiding the beach from us then flattening into white water, gathering up boogie boards and bodysurfers and tumbling them into the sand.

Suddenly a fin broke the surface not far from us. We looked at each other in mutual terror, then at the few other people nearby – who clearly had noticed nothing. We didn't say anything but swam as fast as we could to shore.

We pulled ourselves up in the shallows, adjusted our bathers for modesty, and looked back out to where we'd been.

'It was a fin,' said my sister.

'A shark?'

'A dolphin,' she replied.

'How do you tell the difference?'

'I don't know.'

'I don't know, either.'

'What shall we do?'

'I don't know.'

'We should tell someone.'

'We should. But what if it *was* a dolphin?'

Silence.

'You'd think it would have eaten someone by now if it was a shark.'

'Yeah. It's most likely swum away,' I agreed.

'Want to go back in?'

'Not just yet.'

We went back to our towels, preferring to let all those blissfully ignorant swimmers get mauled to death than for us to be embarrassed and exposed as ignorant pale southerners calling a dolphin a shark.

The screams we were anticipating didn't eventuate. To this day I have no idea if it was a shark.

From then on the water became both a pleasure and a fear, the most blissful place for me, shared by the scariest thing. Look at the beautiful patterns the waves' ripples play on the sand beneath, I'd think. Feel how cool the water is, how enlivening and exhilarating – but what was that? Seaweed, my own shadow, a shark?

So many aspects of our daily lives are contradictory, black and white not always creating grey. Sometimes being bad is at the same time being good. Are you unlucky or lucky when your car dies not far from the mechanic's? Or you trip and break your leg with an ambulance nearby? Don't stress the small stuff, but remember – the devil is in the detail.

I made a short animated film called *Living with Happiness*, in which a happy new mother can't stop having vivid imaginings of that very happiness being shattered, by toaster electrocutions, baby bath drownings, bridges collapsing and jet planes coming through the roof, destroying all. Her happiness is being eroded by her awareness of it and her recognition of its frailty. This mother I created was someone who was probably skydiving and eating raw shellfish pre-baby. In the film she only recovers some equanimity when rescued from an actual life-threatening situation, nearly drowning after being dragged into the water by a freak wave. She is rescued by a nine-year-old boy who tells her, 'The secret is not to panic', and instead of being dumped by another wave, she rides it thrillingly back to shore.

When I was invited to show the film in America, I gladly (but guiltily, leaving my toddler for a week) accepted. Coming out of the screening, an audience member approached me, gave me a little hug, smiled and said, 'I hope you're all right and on medication now.'

Because of the feedback on the film up to that point I had been hoping I had just voiced what thousands of people silently think, and that I was normal. But now, in Aspen, the world's richest town per capita, I had to question whether I was normal or actually a self-indulgent crazy woman, who had clearly put her mental illness on show in a desperate plea for help and attention.

What's normal? Is it an absence of difference? Would I actually *be* normal if I wasn't anxious in these times of knowing too much yet simultaneously not knowing enough? Would I be more or less anxious if I actually had something to be anxious about? Would I be more scared of flying if I'd been involved in a plane crash or less anxious for having survived one?

I obviously needed to write some more – my compulsion to create joined by my newly acquired need for therapy and an effort to get both William and myself a job. I started another film script, a bigger one.

I wrote about all the things that interested me: mortality, slow death, sudden death, fear of death, our ability or lack of ability to control our world, our fate and what everything means. I decided to make it a romantic comedy.

I could have explored these ideas in some exotic location, but I didn't. I had already written two feature films, and both were in the bottom drawer. This one William and I were determined to make, even if we had to act all the parts ourselves. So the film was set near a railway line, in an area with a varied economy and population – basically, our street, because that would be the cheapest location. And I guess because my father's cancer and death had brought up so many questions, I gave the lead character a likely diagnosis on Friday night that he had to deal with pretty much alone until confirmation on the Monday.

I showed the first draft to William, my leading – but unfortunately superstitious – man. 'You've given me cancer! You can't give me cancer!'

'If I give you cancer in the film you won't get it in real life.'

William looked at me, thinking. From here on he had little hope. Maybe I was right and it would protect him from cancer or maybe he was right and it was tempting fate. But here it was, printed on the page. He couldn't un-know it. No wonder people came up with such strict rules in religion – superstition can be exhausting.

'It would be too weird,' I added.

William was still doubtful, mentally struggling.

'But then again, great publicity – if you timed it right.'

William looked at me. 'What?'

'You know, if you got cancer and –'

'I can't believe you said that,' he said, shocked.

'If your character in the film won the lottery you wouldn't think you'd then win. You'd be thinking, Well, that's it, it'll never happen to me now – you can't win the jackpot twice. Just like you wouldn't get cancer.'

We made the film, in the way I imagine most films are made, with a combination of torture, excitement, boredom and surprises. Largely about fate, control and the search for meaning, the film became an exercise in just that.

Soon after we started shooting, one of the child actors broke her arm, and turned up for work in a full wrist-to-shoulder plaster cast. We had already shot her in a swimming-pool scene, arm fine, so we had to write it into the film. It became a wonderful piece of serendipity – for the film's story, not for the poor girl – as it gave the plot a whole new level, people making judgements about something that was essentially no one's fault. Our bad luck became good luck.

Another actor's character – a seven-months-pregnant woman – had some eerily prophetic lines:

> You get this phone call from the hospital saying you've got high blood pressure and they want to induce you, so you spend the next six agonising hours thinking you're going to have a baby smaller than your own hand . . . until they ring and say, 'Oops! Sorry – wrong person!' So you think, Fantastic! Until you realise that is actually happening to someone.'

And it did happen. The actor gave birth to her own baby two days later, premature. We weren't sure whether this had been brought on by the script or the actor believing in the script and taking method acting too far, or it was just a weird coincidence.

Another day we were shooting a scene where the father falls out of bed and his wife can no longer lift him, and they sit on the floor together, knowing that it's over; he will have to go to hospital and there he will die. They cry. It was a harrowing day, and made more harrowing by a key crew member receiving the news that his mother had just died. He flew home and we struggled on without him, dealing in fiction with what he was now dealing with in fact.

It became a bit of a joke on set, who would suffer from the next theme of the film. I distinctly remember someone asking who was going to get run over by a train or get cancer and me saying, 'Bags not the cancer.' Even though I lived by the railway tracks.

We finished shooting and edited the film. I coloured in all the animation drawings over a long Melbourne winter. In the school holidays, William took the kids to see his family in Redcliffe, leaving me to do a couple of weeks of long hours and make some progress. He reported back on sunshine and shows and silliness, and I went to the doctor because my cold wouldn't go away and I felt sorry for myself and wanted to get out of the edit suite for an hour or two.

It was a new doctor and she sent me for an X-ray of my chest, just as a precaution.

I sat in the cubicle where they tell you to wait in your hospital gown and, in my case, odd socks. I read the medical ads placed there to keep the community informed, amused and alarmed, made a mental note to tell the radiographer I wasn't pregnant, to not have multiple sex partners if William ever left me, that ice-cream was at the top of the food pyramid and to check my breasts for lumps. Running out of posters to read, I checked my breasts then and there, following the instructions on the 'how to' poster, I found a lump.

I wasn't overly fussed. I had felt a lump in a similar place before and just been embarrassed when the doctor informed me it was probably the bone and there was no point doing a mammogram, I was too young. Another doctor had said it was doubtful I'd have to worry about breast cancer, as I had small breasts and the lumps couldn't hide. This doctor also didn't hand out antibiotics to the children for every cold they had or 'just in case'. He was no fuss, I liked him, and, as you have to, trusted him.

I went home and had a bath, counting my blessings – not least the peace of having the house to myself. I coughed. I felt my breast. It was definitely a lump. I coughed again. I wanted to be in Queensland.

I went back to the doctor to get the X-ray results. She looked at the pictures silently for a long time, turning the sheet this way and that. This, of course, let me know all was not well. I must have lung cancer. Why else spend so long looking at an X-ray? She was obviously trying to find the words to break the news to me.

In an effort to end the silence and distract her, or at least get her to get on with it and tell me how long I had to live, I told her about the breast lump.

She put the chest X-rays down on her desk, sighed and gestured me up onto the examination table. She felt the lump.

'How is the X-ray result?' I asked.

She kept feeling the lump, replying casually, her eyes averted either from me or my breasts. 'They're not sure. It could be a form of pneumonia or it could be just a shadow in the way they've taken the photo.'

I dared ask, trying to make it sound like a semi-joke, 'Not a shadow as in – cancer?'

She laughed in that, 'Oh, you patients really should stop reading women's magazines and get a grip' kind-doctor way.

'No,' she said. 'And I'm ninety-nine per cent sure that lump isn't either. But we'll send you for a mammogram to put any doubts you have to rest. And put you on antibiotics in case it's pneumonia.'

This was definitely a new doctor. Pneumonia? I didn't even have a temperature. I might try a Panadol first, I thought. Or a glass of wine and a night on the couch watching 'Murder, She Wrote'.

I went for the mammogram. I was expecting it would be the ninety-nine per cent and nothing or an embarrassing cyst caused by an ingrown hair or some other result of a lack of good grooming. My sister had had a lump removed, which hadn't turned out to be anything, and she is very well groomed. We just weren't a high-drama family. For most of our lives, we weren't the sort of people things 'happened' to. None of us had been kidnapped or won the lottery or been in a tsunami or cyclone or married an airline owner. None of us even owned an airline. We were pretty normal.

But then, I guess, even in 'normal' families, someone is eventually going to have a radiographer avoid eye-contact, while requesting another picture 'just to check something'. Cancer is pretty normal, so many people have brushes with it. Perhaps Dad dying at sixty-seven was rude enough to keep the rest of us protected for a while? His parents had been in their late eighties. I was only forty-four. I still had a grandmother.

But no, apparently having a parent with cancer should make you more aware and alarmed, not less. Like bad luck clinging to bad luck.

Not that the mammogram people told me I had cancer. They don't talk about results, unless you definitely don't have cancer. But I asked, 'Have you found anything?'

'The doctor will talk to you.'

'What have you found?'

'The doctor will talk to you.'

'That answer is starting to make me a bit worried.'

'The doctor –' long pause, looking busy '– will talk to you.'

I remembered someone telling me once that if the jury members don't meet the prisoner's eyes when they come to deliver the verdict, the prisoner knows he will hang. I could imagine that to be true. I desperately tried to meet the radiographer's eyes. He took a last image, and I tried small talk, not taking my eyes off his face. 'It's a nice day outside… A bit cold, though I guess it is winter.'

'Mmm. You can get dressed now.'

He turned off the machine, gathered his things, politely avoided any chance of eye-contact and left the room.

I went home. It was Thursday; the doctor would have the results on Friday.

I rang Queensland. They had been busy with their Redcliffe Show entries all day. Stella had entered the garden sculpture and the Anzac biscuits competitions, while Clem was again going against the toughest competitors in the plain scones challenge. Auntie Lol was putting in her famous marmalade, Iris some eggs and William was defending his title with the one loaf of bread he baked every year. They would know their results on Friday. Ah, we were indeed a family.

I don't know if I would have mentioned the mammogram, but I had no choice as all the show preparation information was given pretty much simultaneously with William shouting, the music up loud, a squabble over bowl-licking and Iris singing a different song in the background as the dogs barked along.

So instead, I exchanged a dozen 'I love you's and hung up. It was very quiet. I poured myself a big glass of wine, made some toast, turned the television back on and kept colouring in the animation for the film.

Friday morning I called the doctor from work to see if they had the results. They hadn't come in yet. Twenty phone calls and much searching for images later, they found them. It was 6 p.m.

The doctor made me an appointment for Monday morning.

'Monday? Why can't you just tell me over the phone?'

'I think it's better you come in. I've moved other people to get you the first appointment on Monday.'

'You've moved people? Why move people? Tell me now!'

'I'm sorry. You really need to come in.'

'Sorry? You can't leave me with that! What am I supposed to do all weekend? You've virtually told me it's bad news. What if it's not as bad news as I'm imagining? What if I kill myself before Sunday night, unable to live with the uncertainty?'

She sighed. 'Can you come in now?'

I drove to the clinic, crawling through Friday-night traffic. Supposedly my last unknowing time. Yet knowing. So why the desperation to know? I guess hope is a pretty strong little bugger.

They were waiting in the dimly lit waiting area, the doctor and the receptionist who'd also stayed back. They were very nice. They told me that it wouldn't be confirmed until biopsy, but they were ninety-nine per cent sure I had breast cancer. It was a large tumour that had been clinging to the chest wall. They didn't know if it would spread, or what would happen next. The specialist would tell me. And thus, like my father before me, I was ushered through the gateway of general practice to the parallel universe of Medical World.

It's not as if I didn't know how this was all going to pan out. I had, after all, just written it, shot it and nearly finished editing it. Why did I have to live it? Some kind of retrospective research demand to make sure I had got William's character's story right? I couldn't change the film now even if I'd got it wrong. And like the lead female character says, just because you know the stages of grief, you don't get out of having to live through them.

I was going to have to go through all that stuff my character had gone through. I would be simultaneously petrified and yet feeling exactly the same way I had the day before, the only difference being I would know something I hadn't known the day before. And that knowing opens up a thousand more questions and acres of ignorance.

I had directed William to play the character as if he were being dumped by a massive wave – tumbled about, swimming frantically towards the surface, only to hit the seabed breathless and panicking – at the same time as being in a state of calm normality. And maybe because I had written it, or maybe because that's how it always goes, that's how the weekend was for me.

I rang Queensland. The usual clamour answered the phone. They had won prizes. Stella's garden-made interpretation of Redcliffe had taken out first prize – she had won five dollars! William had again won for his bread, even though this year there was one other entry. Clem had been given an encouragement award from the fiercely competitive elderly-lady scone-making committee – a cookbook. Auntie Lol's marmalade had proven to be too rustic and chunky – and in my opinion delicious – to win anything. Iris had forgotten to take up the eggs and thought the whole thing was silly anyway. And rigged. They had bought me a show-bag and gone on the Cha-Cha ride for me.

I didn't tell them my results. What was the point? I hadn't told them I'd entered anything. Why tell them I didn't win? Why interrupt their happiness so they would rush down and be miserable and questioning in the cold with me? Especially for what would hopefully be the breast cancer equivalent of a mole removal.

Not quite.

But, being lucky as well as unlucky, the lung shadow did turn out to be a bad photo, not the spread of breast cancer. And though it was in my lymph system it was still considered early-stage breast cancer, a sometimes curable disease. I had a mastectomy then six months of chemotherapy. They make you stick to the regime by emphasising that if it comes back, there is no cure and it is fatal. It is a leap of faith. One minute you have a sorry-for-yourself-because-you're-not-in-Queensland cold, and the next, on the advice of a few people in offices and vague-looking black-and-white images, you are getting one of your breasts cut off and poisoning your body for six months. And poisoning yourself when healthy is weird – it's like every cell in your body is shouting at you, 'Wrong!' It's sick-making, hair-loss-making and exhausting. But it has an end point and that gives you a focus, an aim, and even a sense of pride when you make it through.

I kept working on the film while I had the treatment and they were finished about the same time, each a good distraction from the other, and together a good distraction from the real problem about to hit me – the flatness every director feels after finishing a film, when four years of intense creativity, where every minute of your life is spent thinking or doing something about your project, dwindles to nothing. A well-earned rest you've forgotten how to have alongside Medical World saying 'Good luck' as it sends you back to your planet.

Two major things completed. What now?

Statistics. I was never good at maths, so this was obviously a gentle reminder that not only should I not have done whatever it was I did to get breast cancer (jury still out) but that I should have paid more attention at school. Is a seventy-five per cent chance of no recurrence in five years good? Sounds good until you imagine it in terms of planes. Would you get on a plane if one in every four was going to plummet out of the sky? Would you swim in the ocean if one in every four people were eaten by sharks? And it gets trickier with the variables.

Working on the basis that I was either dumb or shell-shocked – or both – my oncologist drew little diagrams with a hundred Sarahs exactly like me. While he was drawing, I was already off in a world where there are a hundred Sarahs living all the lives I could have led. Some more likely than the one I'm actually leading. Others, fantasies that would involve a personality transplant to achieve. There's Sarah, fat and happy, hiring little boats to tourists. There's Sarah with four kids on the farm, stepping over puppies and preserving peaches. There's the lawyer Sarah, gunning for human rights. And then there's the Sarah I love a lot, the quiet, pretty one who found the cure for cancer a year or so ago.

So, seventy-five Sarahs, who all undertook the same treatment, were likely to walk through the oncologist's door for their appointments in five years' time. I could imagine them all, jostling about, trying to count each other, standing close to the door in case there were seventy-six or seventy-seven in the waiting room and they had to dash to make the cut. Some of them with their laptops, some taking the opportunity to catch up on reading *House and Garden*, or what Britney's up to. Some with partners or kids who wanted to come. A great big party of Sarahs at the five-year mark, even though twenty-five of them – the unluckiest ones – are dead or battling a recurrence. And a recurrence, of course, is 'incurable' and 'fatal'.

In most cancers if you make the five-year mark you're a survivor. But in my type and stage of breast cancer it would never go away. There would be fewer Sarahs showing up each year, like a small-town World War II parade.

Percentages and statistics don't actually apply to you. You can't really get all those Sarahs to stand still and behave the same. At least one of them is going to sneak off and eat cake or become a heroin addict. We had a one in ten thousand chance of Cosmo dying the way he did. Yet we couldn't win the lottery or a raffle, even when we bought half the tickets.

And thus begins the mental struggle. How to live with this percentaged potential for a shorter life? It's the sort of mind mess that every smoker should be in every time they light up. Or every mountain climber, sky diver or driver. Let's face it, every day in Australia four people who get in their cars aren't going to come home and more than double that will be seriously injured. How often does that give us pause before we whip up to the supermarket for ice-cream?

But those kinds of odds feel different, and things do change with a diagnosis like mine. Either that or I am a neurotic bore or, of course, as usual, both.

People often say any one of us could be run over by a bus any day, we all have to die. But when you can see the bus, and know what colour it is, its horsepower, the number of passengers on board and when it's likely to arrive, it's more troubling. I was certainly troubled, also shocked, upset and cross. And questioning everything. Why? Why did I get this? Followed by: What can I do to make it stay away? How can I get some control in this world?

Having friends of many different faiths, I explored quite a few of them. I clutched cloths blessed by bishops, searched the lawns with my daughter for four-leaved clovers, listened to meditation tapes, thought positively and tried to be calm and not care, knowing I have another life and all that's meant to be, will be.

But coming from hearty stock who know that anything you enjoy can't be good for you, I knew I had to give up all the things I like and that, obviously, if they don't know what causes breast cancer, it's going to be ice-cream, wine, chips or chocolate – not asbestos, pesticides, random viruses or genetic malfunction.

I have a friend who went through the same experience. She is younger, fitter, a life-long teetotaller and vegan. We chatted about what we thought caused our cancers. She told me she thought it was the peanut butter. I couldn't believe it. 'Peanut butter? That's all you've got?'

To be on the safe side, I added it to my 'no' list. I gave up all added sugar and salt, dairy and processed food, which, believe me, doesn't leave a lot. I bent the rules slightly to leave red wine on the 'yes' list. I have more than a dozen collected articles telling me it can cure cancer, which I keep near my bedside for the middle-of-the-night doubt hours.

I lasted two years, only breaking when Stella made me a cake. When I said, 'That's lovely, but I won't have any, thanks, darling,' tears came to her eyes. She had tried so hard.

'I made it with dark chocolate. Eighty per cent.'

I looked at her then at the cake – a packet one, full of cheap margarine and hydrogenated oils, messily draped in thick green-and-yellow icing and untidily decorated with cheap sweets. What was I thinking? I ate three pieces, the third with ice-cream.

I was not alone in blaming myself for my cancer. Either deliberately or in trying to be helpful, many people blame you. Or themselves, if they love you enough. William spent quite a while worrying that he had brought it on through irritating me, sometimes deliberately.

And, in the way we do, people try to distance themselves from nasty, mortal things. Oh, those Philippines ferries – of course they go down, they're just old rust buckets. Oh, those tsunamis – people die because they don't have sufficient building regulations in those countries. Oh, that cancer – you know she used to smoke/drink/eat sugar/hold in her anger/swim in chlorinated pools and eat smoked salmon.

You're allowed to get a cold, measles or tinea, but cancer – that's witches-of-Salem stuff. It needs a cause and with lack of a cause . . . Well, sorry, we just have to blame you. People tell you to stay positive, that it's all in your head. Have you tried almond kernels? The juice diet? Meditation retreats? Were you stressed?

Answer? Not really, not until I got cancer. Now it's pretty tricky trying to exert control over my whole world as well as accepting I have absolutely *no* control and that I am totally insignificant in the universe, at the same time as being so hugely important to my family, particularly the children and the dog. Who would feed them?

At Sea

Sarah

Our film, *Look Both Ways*, was very successful. William and I both got to travel to places we'd never been. Not difficult, as there is no film festival in Redcliffe. It was a wonderful experience, though perhaps one best enjoyed when you are twenty-four and childless or in your fifties and sixties with children who don't miss you. The trips and opportunities we turned down would make either of those age-groups weep. I felt this way myself, but that's the way it goes. We both would have preferred the success to come without the related – or unrelated – price tag of cancer, but we knew it was sweeter and more intense for it. Like swimming in a pool that actually has a shark in it, you don't take the pleasure for granted. Life was good, and we knew it.

I met a filmmaker at the New Zealand film festival. We had seen each other's films, which is always a relief. He was a lovely guy, who I'd heard had had cancer when finishing his first feature. He'd heard of my being in a similar boat so, after a polite start, we were soon deep in sharing cancer and filmmaking war stories, admiration for each other's work and a bottle of wine, which we both hesitated momentarily about, then drank happily anyway.

I asked him whether he thought filmmaking had brought on his cancer.

'Yes, of course,' he said.

Uh? I had been expecting – and wanting – a different answer, one that would let me go on and feel confident about making another film.

'This is my second run – my first cancer I was diagnosed during the completion of my short film,' he explained.

Oh.

'Then nothing, no cancer, then another film in the can, and there's the cancer back again.'

'So would you risk another film?' I ventured.

'Yes,' he said firmly.

'Even though you think it brings on the cancer?'

'Yes,' he said. 'I like filmmaking that much. It's my life, it's everything.'

I guess filmmaking is stressful. Other people's money, trust and effort dependent on you to pull off something only one in ten experienced cashed-up Hollywood producers manage to do. Add to that the fact it's a one-shot career – stuff it up and you're a kitchen hand again – and that by the time you start working on it you have probably already invested four years of your time, money and often your fee just to get it over the line, then it can indeed be a tad stressful.

Leaving your children with relatives for months and missing your daughter's first day of school to work eighteen-hour days with barely time for a phone call, never mind for listening to your body. Answering a thousand questions each day, only occasionally having any idea whether the whole film's success rests on your answer. A successful film is, I think, the result of not making a single error from start to finish plus a healthy amount of sheer luck. If the script isn't right, the film will never be. If the casting isn't right, ditto. If the performances aren't believable, if they can't sustain the audience's belief and attention, ditto again. The edit, the music, the art direction, the wardrobe, the props, the locations, the lot – ditto. By the end of the shoot you can't even tell someone if you want a glass of red or white wine to celebrate, the decision is just too hard.

So yes, a tad stressful. But not real stress. Real stress is living in a war zone with two disabled children, no respite, not enough food, an abusive father and really bad psoriasis. Filmmaking is a luxury and a choice and, on the whole, addictive and fun. And like for an Olympian distance swimmer, it's just a whole lot of quiet lonely work for four years, until, if you're lucky and uninjured and at your peak, you might be able to get the gang back together and go for it.

So would I want to make another film? Would it be tempting fate? Do I have that level of power over life events? Of course not.

These days I'm basically a mother and homemaker with a creative compulsion. Homemaking is pushing it, really. Most of my life is spent competing with William as to who is the biggest creative diva and therefore does the least housework. So, not even having power over a vacuum cleaner, I don't see why I would have any power over future events. Even those involving myself.

But then, maybe I do. If I never go near the road, it will be pretty hard for a bus to hit me. And maybe it's no accident that good luck and bad luck circle around me in equal proportions, that things I imagine to be true are proven true, not because my imagination is very normal and therefore universal, but because I do actually cause these things. Maybe I have a super-power?

Perhaps it's best for sanity not to follow that line of thinking.

I had been hoping Hollywood would call and ask me to make *Jaws: The Prequel*, so I didn't have to write another one myself. But when that failed to eventuate and someone else got *Anaconda 2*, I realised I would have to write another film. Most people write their first film around thinly disguised autobiographical stories about their most important life events. Here I was, wondering about cancer, metaphysics and mortality, yet I'd already made that film, dammit. And if I made it about my actual journey, all the new questions . . . Who wants to spend fifteen dollars and an hour and a half watching a bald scared woman not eat ice-cream or potato chips and chewing her nails over whether her cancer will come back?

Pre my cancer discovery, we had a Christmas cocktails-and-chips party. My good friend Therese, who lives around the corner, had helped me set up the backyard with coloured lights and decorations. She went home to get changed and walked back with some friends, one of whom is a doctor whose brother had died from a cerebral aneurism. Therese bent to fix her shoe, stood back up and mentioned she had a strange sensation in her head, a sort of headache. She was all for still coming, thinking a strawberry daiquiri would sort her out, but was persuaded to go to the hospital. Just to be on the safe side.

Once they got there, Therese collapsed with a burst aneurism. What amazingly good luck, we all thought as we hoped first that she wouldn't die, then that she wouldn't be a vegetable, then that she would walk again, talk again, make sense when she talked. Or, then again, what awful luck – she missed a party and she almost died.

When Therese thankfully recovered, everyone else was saying, 'Thank God that's over, let's get back to normality,' but Therese was just starting to assimilate what had happened, having been unconscious during everyone else's journey. Her questioning was a lot like mine, but her story way more exciting.

Therese liked the idea of her story being a film. Like me now, she avidly reads anything about her particular disease, and was happy to add her story to the resource pile. As well as writing Therese's story and exploring all our questions, I made sure – after the life-imitating-film experience of the first feature – that in this second script, everyone would be good and nice, live happily ever after and win the lottery. I also made it a romantic comedy.

After three or four years of writing and financing, we got to make the film. The fear of my cancer returning was declining, the vacuum being neatly filled by the fear of film-making and stuffing things up.

But all went pretty well. Nobody seemed to become who they had played, or suffer what their character suffered. William played a six-foot-four transvestite, but hasn't taken it up as a hobby as far as I know.

We edited with the same team and I got a bit nervous, reaching the same point as when I had been diagnosed before. I had a cold but didn't go to the doctor, playing it safe. We would be able to travel the world and go to parties and enjoy its success. But then, of course, *My Year Without Sex* wasn't a festival film. We hardly got invited anywhere. All that health and nothing to squander it on.

But we did get invited to the New Zealand film festival again. I sent an email to my dinner friend, saying, 'Let's catch up.' I didn't hear back, then after a while heard that he was very ill and unlikely to recover. He didn't. It was really sad. I had particularly

wanted to see his next film, compare notes again, share a bottle of wine again. I wanted him to have a long life making great things. And, of course, like everyone who hears of their peers dying, I didn't want it to be me. Having the same or a similar disease, you get the double selfish stab – I find it impossible to think only of the sick or dead person, I also think of myself. Definitely not even a minor saint.

I went to New Zealand. William was already there, making a film, and we were in Auckland for a few nights together. A rare thing without children. We had a lovely energetic and happy reunion in which I hurt my rib. I will leave you to decide for yourselves what activity we were enjoying at the time, but he is a lovely man and I'm not into kick-boxing or hanging from lightshades, but will confess there was an excellent bottle of duty-free champagne involved.

I clutched my side as we made jokes about our clumsiness, our weight, our middle-aged-ness. It hurt to laugh, so it was hilarious. For a couple of weeks it seemed everybody was making the best jokes as I held my ribs, begging them not to make me laugh. There was no real point going to the doctor. I knew, even if it was broken, there wouldn't be much to do except avoid laughing, really.

It seemed as if it was getting better, then one of the chooks jumped on William's head, and his reaction was so big and out of proportion we all cracked up. Me, literally. He was hilarious – had us in tears of laughter, and for me, pain.

This was a little worrying. Surely ribs don't just break like that? But I pushed that thought aside. I don't know how. Perhaps the chemical menopause I'd been sitting in for five years had stripped me not only of oestrogen, but of all ability to multitask, so now I too was like my boyfriends of the past who could honestly say they hadn't thought to ring me as they were eating lunch or doing up their shoelaces or something of equally focused intensity.

We tempted fate further and had a five-years-clear, happy-to-be-here party. And I was here and happy – definitely on earth and, most of the time, at the party. But, like a pokie player who doesn't take the jackpot home, we had pushed our luck.

I went to my regular oncologist's check-up. I mentioned my rib, when he noticed me wince after laughing at his joke, not wanting him to think it was that bad a joke.

Then it was back to the cubicles, and back to Medical World. I had a recurrence.

It was different from being told the first time. The first time – the early breast cancer – I felt a heightened anxiety and hyper-awareness of the many levels, meanings and fragility of the world around me and inside me. This second time I felt more of a sleepiness, a drowsy awakening, a gentle prod. Of course, the rib had some cancer in it, that's why it hadn't got better. Of course William isn't that heavy, and our reunion hadn't been *that* acrobatic, though it had been funny.

I don't know if I had spent the last five years expecting it and so it wasn't such a shock, or whether I went via shock to denial so quickly I didn't notice. Or I ceased worrying because I had no further need to – it was here, the worst had happened.

On my twenty-first birthday, I was camping with friends on Fraser Island. We were at least eight kilometres from the nearest shop, but to celebrate my friend Chrissie and I decided to walk the distance to buy Paddle Pops. I had had a craving for one for days. For a chocolate Paddle Pop.

The wide beach was deserted that day, with only the ubiquitous four-wheel drive tracks carving through the sand to tell us there were other people in the world. It was warm with clear blue skies and sparkling water.

We walked until we were too hot and the water too tempting. We dumped excess clothes and shoes and waded in. I stopped. I thought I saw a fin. I jumped through the next wave and called to Chrissy, 'Did you see that? Was it a fin?'

'You see fins everywhere,' Chrissie pointed out. 'Every day.'

True. Though, in my defence, I do actually see real fins. Once there was a small shark in a sea pool I was about to swim in. I saw dolphins on a whale-watch cruise.

But we both paused, now waist-deep in seawater, and looked. I thought I saw a glimpse of a fin further out. No curve of body. Chrissy still didn't see it.

Then, both of us watching, the swell ahead of us rose into a clear wave, with a perfect solid and silhouetted area the shape of a shark. A big shark, longer and heavier than either of us, swimming parallel to the beach.

We both ran back to shore, laughing and squealing, as excited as much as surprised and scared.

We walked along, following the shark, appearing and disappearing in the waves. Then we saw two at once and squealed again. Then three, four, six, ten, a dozen big sharks, trapped in the channel. It was thrilling.

We watched for a while, then kept walking, seeing the same or more sharks, we weren't sure. It was still so hot. At first we ventured back in to ankle depth, to splash some water over ourselves, jumping back to land as soon as a shark appeared. Then to our knees. Then we lay down in two inches of water, to try to get our bodies wet and cool.

Still a kilometre from the store and busting to really swim we came up with a plan. One of us would keep our eyes out, make sure the sharks stayed at least five metres away, while the other ducked under. I watched Chrissy do it. She came up fast, but laughing, exhilarated. My turn. I hesitated, looked around, took in a big breath and ducked. The moment was exquisite. A hot head cooled, the beautiful clear water and the roller-coaster, scary-movie thrill of the sharks nearby.

Soon we were both in and swimming. Not deep, but in. I guess we had got used to the sharks and so we weren't too afraid. They didn't seem that interested in us anyway, they were there for the fish, waiting for the tide to turn. We didn't invade their space and they didn't invade ours. We were euphoric. We were swimming with sharks!

Later, on the same walk, we came across a group of men with a Range Rover and a winch, having 'caught' one of the trapped sharks. They were heaving it in through the shallows and it was putting up an epic struggle. I was reminded, as I internally barracked for the shark, of the unfairness of the statistics in the shark–human relationship. They kill maybe five or six of us a year in the whole world. We eat thousands of them as fish and chips just in our own suburb.

I would never enter water with a shark warning sign but once I was in there, swimming with sharks, it was just that – the fear was less than the fact. The broken ribs were not warning signs. They were the sharks. Quiet little confirmation sharks. I don't have to fear cancer anymore. I have it.

It's like in the film *Jaws*, my personal favourite monster movie. It's supposed to be scariest when that famous music plays, warning you the shark is nearby and someone is vulnerable. But the scariest part for me is when we aren't expecting the shark because the music doesn't warn us.

I watched it by myself in a large cinema, a treat for my birthday. A man sat down right in front of me and I was too embarrassed to either ask him to move or move myself. So I sat there and endured his size as well as his verbal tough-man commentary. 'Tch, that's not scary!', 'Ooh, here comes the nasty big shark!', 'It doesn't even look real!'

I don't know why some people feel compelled to ruin others' experience, but it was a joyful moment when, without warning, the hero dived underwater in the near dark and a severed head rolled down to face him. Tough man nearly hit the roof in fear then shut up for the remainder of the film.

The cancer is here, the *Jaws* music has stopped and apart from a still-broken rib, I feel pretty much the same.

I had been one of the Sarahs to make it back to the oncologist's room after five years without a recurrence, along with the other seventy-four. But now we have a new hundred Sarahs, all of whom have metastasised cancer. Advanced cancer. The incurable and eventually fatal one, and not a lot of us are going to be back in five years' time.

Some of the new Sarahs were in tears in the waiting room, occasionally sobbing, wailing, 'It's not fair.' Some just stared at a plant, possibly thinking how beautiful it was and wondering whether they would see it flower another year. One or two were trying to see the bright side – no more exercise tapes or housework; this Sarah wins the creative-diva war with William. Some were saying, 'There's no way I will have chemo again, I just can't.' Others were saying, 'I'll do whatever they want.' How could you not? Your life is not your own, not really. You just have to do whatever it takes to stay as long as you can. Those Sarahs were in the majority.

So here was a rep of the new Sarahs, sitting in the doctor's room with her younger sister. We had one of those sessions that you can either imagine or have seen in movies. And even when you're there, in the scene, it still feels dreamlike and as if everybody is acting.

I asked the doctor, 'How long without treatment?'

'Six, twelve, maybe eighteen months,' he replied, looking only at my sister.

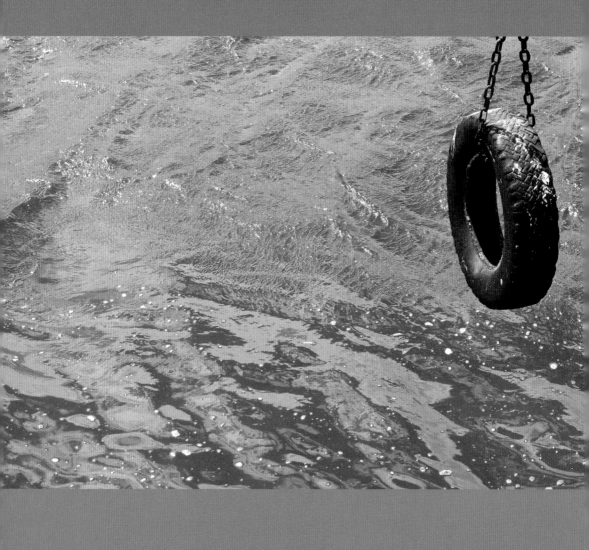

Pause, get new tissues, try and make voice not tremble.

'And with treatment?'

'Maybe double that,' he said, again to my poor sister.

It sounds like a game: You have two years to live, what will you do?

After finishing reading those a-thousand-things-you-must-see/do/watch/go to books, you probably only have one year left to actually do anything. So what would you do? Some people have ready answers, like if they won the lottery. They'd give this much to these people, buy a new car, donate this much to charity. And with the limited life? I'd want to see this place, one last time. I'd want to see these people again. I've always wanted to go to Paris/skydive/do French-cooking classes/be a roller-derby queen. But would they? Would they really want to, nevermind actually do? They say that a lot of people who win the lottery don't even quit their jobs, nevermind change their lives. And I guess a lot of people who only have a limited time to live spend it pretty much full-time in Medical World.

I don't want to do that. And, fortunately, I still don't feel very sick. It doesn't even hurt so much when I laugh. And things are just as funny. A gecko got inside William's shirt when we were in a crowded restaurant with the kids not long ago. We laughed for hours. I don't really want to see people or go anywhere – you can't do everything and I've done as much as I haven't done. I don't want a bucket list. I just want my life that I love for as long as possible.

I once took the kids to the Scienceworks opening of 'Eaten Alive', a museum exhibition about things that can eat you. I'm sure there's a more technical term for that, but it escapes me. There were giant spiders, boa constrictors, a large shark and, most important of all, Val Taylor. Val Taylor, being an early advocate for sharks, was a bit of a heroine of mine. I vicariously dived with her through her career, me being a mere snorkeller and shallows swimmer in reality. We paused at the same time in front of the giant spider. I smiled a stranger's smile. As I had only the beginnings of hair regrowth, it wasn't surprising that she recognised I had cancer, but it was a little surprising that she said to me, straight up, 'You've had cancer.'

I confessed it was so. Having cancer hadn't been far from my mind – an 'Eaten Alive' exhibition does tend to remind you that technically you are enduring just that.

She looked me in the eye, paused then said, 'You've got to keep busy. Have something you have to do – it works.' Then she walked away.

Keep busy. Yes, good advice. Sitting around soon leads to lying around, which shortly afterwards becomes the foetal position with my head under the covers.

I had always told myself that the minute I knew the cancer had come back, or if for some other reason I was given notice on my life, that I would sort my photographs. I have so many. I took too many on film, and now, with digital, it's an embarrassment – twenty-five shots just to capture the best moment of a baby's laugh. But then do you select the one shot and delete the rest? Of course not – how could you delete any photos of your beautiful babies? Try tearing up a printed photograph of your child – it's really hard, it feels wrong. It's worse than throwing out the Mum-knitted jumper that you haven't worn for ten years.

If I leave the photos where they are – prints, negs and discs sitting around in endless shoeboxes – any sane person would pick out ten, maybe twenty, and throw out the rest without looking at them, because to look at them would be like watching a real-time documentary, taking almost as long as the life itself took.

But if they were in curated albums, books of visual home stories, what wonderful things to leave behind for all those who want to spend a little time in past times, in other places – holidays, birthdays and Christmases when all the old gang were still around. I do it often at my mother's house. She is a good person and collated hers as the photos came in.

But to make them now – how? Apart from choosing between subject, chronological or theme order, there's the problem of who they're for if they're not for me.

Knowingly pasting a photograph of yourself with an old boyfriend into an album you will leave to your husband and children just doesn't feel right. And that one of you smoking in your youth? Let's just pop that one in the bin. And get rid of any that make me look fat, cross, badly dressed or tipsy. Is this the kind of editing to do? Try to erase anything that doesn't suit who I'd like to be today? Even though all that came before has created who I am now?

But so much, if not already erased, is unimportant to me now. I can truly say that every year I've had has been better than the one before. I may have regrets, but I've never wanted to go back to any other year or time.

My life is so much now about the last twenty years with William, twenty years in the same house together. That's longer than I lived with my parents, ten times longer than any share house. Longer than anything except maybe a couple of seemingly indestructible friendships. Twenty years during which we could have moved or broken up, but never did. Sometimes through inertia or a lack of time, more often through actually liking each other, and liking our house. And the loveliness of honeymoon periods after times of not liking each other so much, when we would find each other again. Not through 'work' or counselling – though I'm sure that both those would have been helpful at various stages – but through the shared organising, or lack of organising, of the lives of four people. And through absences that were long enough to miss each other, through the love of our children and seeing each other in them. So many things, really, to keep us together. Shared likes and dislikes: short-term politics (dislike), noodles and chilli (like), murder mysteries (like), housework (dislike), our children (love).

Our children.

How do you go about telling them that everything might spiral out of control and you will have to leave them, and that Dad will most likely be a grumpy mess? Why potentially wreck their lives now with anxiety if you are going to have another five years or ten? But what if it is months? How can you leave them open to shock and feelings of betrayal that you didn't tell them?

How much do they know already? Perhaps it is like sex education – when you think you should bring them up to speed, they either look at you aghast, cover their ears and run away singing loudly in case a single word catches them, or say, 'Yeah, it's fine, Mum. It's all good,' in a voice that makes you think they may actually know more than you.

They can still surprise me by being both more resilient and more needy than I would have thought. And I make myself sick thinking of them calling me, needing me, and me not being there. And yet me being there doesn't really help much sometimes.

I don't know when I will have to go. I give myself small aims: get through the summer, get through the winter. See Clem finish school. Get Stella to the stage when her friends are as important to her as I am. But I don't believe it's in my control. I have seen the most excellent and deserving people do their absolute best to control their own biology and fail. I would feel a fake and a traitor to them if I thought it was up to me. Cancer's a disease, and good people die.

It's all about the medicine now. Some treatments have failed, some have worked for a while, like the one I have now, and hopefully it will be working for a long while longer. And I am, of course, lucky.

Lucky to live in Australia, with a public health system that for me has been wonderful, lucky to have such a popular cancer in breast cancer, one that has touched so many that so many others are dedicated not only to finding a cure, but to making life so much better for those of us lugging it around. When each of my treatments has failed, there has been another one waiting for me to try. I love medical research now. Now I *want* medical trials; even if I get the placebo or the trial comes to nothing, it might just help me and it might just help others. Vale, Cosmo.

My oncologist doesn't talk much about the hundred Sarahs anymore. They are all a bit frazzled, taking drugs, unsteady when their eyes are closed, a little prone to tears and black jokes. He just gives me each new drug by telling me about the people who have done the best on it. There's always a real person who's still walking into his rooms smiling and healthy after a year, three years. And they were always sicker than me when they started. Then, when that medication fails for me or stalls the cancer's progress for a lesser time than was hoped, he doesn't mention that person again. Instead, he has a new person on the new drug who still walks smiling into his office after a year.

I don't mind if he does it to keep the hope alive or to get me through the day. Ultimately, I do have to get through the day, and though sometimes I want to shout and scream and sob that it's not fair, I can't. Because, after five minutes, it would be very boring for me, make the time my family has with me a bore, and because it's not really true.

How do you measure a 'fair share' of time? By quantity or quality? Mine has been of excellent quality. I've had a great time. I didn't spend twenty-five years in a job I hate, resenting it but needing it. I've never been confined to a wheelchair. I'm not deaf or blind. And I'm not twenty-five. I'm about the same age as the life expectancy of someone born in Cameroon. In a few more years I'll be pushing at the life expectancy of Indigenous Australians. A real tragedy.

I'm not a tragedy. I can't complain. I've had it good. The best thing I can do is balance the good luck with the bad and go with good grace or, in the current parlance of my children, suck it up and get on with what I have to do with what I've got. And I have a lot. As well as a loving husband, children, wider family, a job I love and enough money to get to Queensland this winter, I also have 'stuff'. Stuff I don't know what to do with. Stuff that belongs only to me, either by meaning or provenance. But I will leave things to my children, and they will, if they are anything like me, leave them scattered through share houses and with temporary lovers and end up with not much. Do I leave my grandmother's engagement ring to Clem? It seems weird to leave it to William, though I am sure he will have another life with another, hopefully nice and older-child loving, woman. I doubt she would want something from my past. Do I mind if it ends up on some girl whom my son is passionately obsessed with for two weeks before moving on to the next love of his life? I don't know. But I wouldn't want him not to know what he was giving away.

I feel like writing on the back of everything we own. 'This is the little picture I bought at the Proserpine Show, when Clem went on his first Cha-Cha ride with me. He loved it. Nanna Anna was there, we had our shadow portraits done. Stella had on a pink parka. We ate real chips made from potatoes.' Or, 'I haven't thrown this vase out, even though I think it's without any aesthetic or monetary value, because my nanna left it to me; she had one leg shorter than the other and always wore a built-up shoe and had the big wide mouth I inherited.'

I won't do it and I don't think I should try to control the meaning of things in the future. And thinking too much about what has been, and what is to come is too heartbreaking. I'd only be halfway through writing up the first drawer of stuff before I was a wreck.

Like my dad's job and personality I seem to have been a dam builder. I am full of all that I have collected, done, loved and regretted. It is a large dam. And I don't want it to crack.

I don't want myself to spill out in some huge tsunami of confusion, memories, half knowledge and grief. Because if it spilled now it would be grief. At another time, drunk at a party with friends, it might have been a spillage of funny and embarrassing stories, but right now everything is tinged with sadness at all that has passed and will pass. I guess when you know you are likely to die you have to grieve before the event. That grief is all right within me, because the measure of it equals how wonderful everything has been and still is.

Some days that's fine, others, less so.

Sometimes the presence of the shark that will deal the final fatal blow feels too close and collides with a fragile moment of one of my children baring their thin-skinned youth and need for their mother. Then the panic rises in me, all my resolve to convey a calm acceptance is thrown overboard and I hold them and we cry. Or I hold them, hold it in, go to the toilet and then cry.

Why do we search for and expect happiness all the time, like some dumb weekend magazine article? Or even contentment. Sometimes rage is good. There are things to be enraged about in this world. There are tears that should fall.

I always liked that saying that you should live every day as if it's your last and simultaneously as if you have twenty more years. I like it in the same way you have to live simultaneously being lucky and unlucky, good and bad, happy and sad.

And when the time does come? I'm lucky that my death will be most likely a simple thing and cause a simple grief. A disease taking me without my permission. No suicide, no ugly divorce fall-out, no angry lost family. A simple straightforward death my sensible plain forebears would be proud of, hopefully followed by a party my naughty convict ancestors would be happy to attend. Hopefully someone will stand on a chair and quote irrelevant poetry.

And my actual death? I'm sure I'll panic at the time. It is even listed as one of the symptoms of near death, along with anxiety and toes turning up. It is surely the body and mind doing what they have been programmed at a cellular level to do – not die.

It's a tricky thing to plan and, like many a birth plan, I'm sure it often goes wrong. My first plan was to do it in my own time in order to skip the dreaded anxious painful panic. I was going to wait until I was unable to go on, until it was very close, and then I'd load myself up on painkillers and go snorkelling, gradually falling asleep, watching gorgeous fish swim near me, the corals, the light diffusing into near purples from greens in the deep patches. And then, when fully asleep, I'd barely notice that I was breathing water not air, like a baby in the womb, and I'd drift away, donating my body to the ocean and its residents, cycles and patterns.

I told William of this plan.

'How would you get to the Barrier Reef?'

'How do you know I was thinking of the Barrier Reef?'

He knows me too well, of course – I don't like the cold water. This was just a sadder version of my annual winter holiday fantasy, the day ending in a gentle departure rather than a strawberry daiquiri.

'If you're so close to the end, how will I get you on the plane? Or to the reef? Are you expecting I'd take you?'

'No, you couldn't come. I could go out to Reefworld.'

'They'd count everyone and find you and rescue you and you'd end up lonely and eating jelly and mince in a Cairns hospital, covered in jellyfish stings.'

Never one to give up an argument easily, I pointed out that I like hospital food and plane food – the little dividing containers and not having to cook it myself.

Of course I wouldn't do it. If I had the strength to snorkel, I'd have the strength to smile and watch my family and friends swim and swirl around me, and I'll take that as long as possible.

I hope when the time comes I'll be at home. I love our house. Somehow the years of Band-Aid renovations and neglect have gelled into a wonderful place to live. It's probably a bit of a dump to some or a castle to others, but for me it's a light-filled container full of people I love.

Maybe I'll be sitting lazily on the back verandah in the sun, next to the window I made from sea-washed glass. Maybe I'll be thinking about the sea, in all its moods, or maybe looking at the afternoon light through the trees we planted here twenty years ago. William will be there, and offer me a cup of tea, and when he's up making it, I'll drift off into a nap, then into the longest nap. And William will bring the tea back and it won't be so bad.

The last time we went swimming, this last summer, the four of us swam out towards a pontoon, a couple of hundred metres from shore. We were halfway there, in deep water, when Clem stopped. 'I thought I saw a fin.'

We were all treading water, looking around. The pontoon was closer than the shore.

'I want to go back,' said Stella.

Then she saw a dark shape near her in the water and nearly climbed up on William's head in an effort to remove herself from the sea. I saw the rounded back, then another as a dolphin leapt out of the water not far from us.

'Dolphins!' we all yelled in unison.

They are bigger than you'd think, dolphins. Especially when they come right up beside you. They dived around us, in their element, their family of three wrapping itself around our family of four. The baby nudged me and dived under Stella. She shrieked. We were all a little scared and cautious but thrilled. Us anyway, I'm not sure about the dolphins. But they followed us to the pontoon. I swam like I had as a teenager – weightless, graceful, exhilarated and so alive. It was one of the best moments in the most romantic year of my life. And it's not over yet.

The kids are just home from school, it's family DVD night. The dog is barking at William. We have to make chocolate banana bread and find a footy boot and get the washing in before it rains. And while despair and disappointment may sit quietly in the corner of the house, hope and grace take up more room. And, again in the parlance of my children, it's all good.

A Walk in the Park

William

One night near the end of the year I went walking around the local footy oval.
I was in a grump. I don't know why; maybe it was the time of year, maybe all the things
that hadn't gone my way during the last twelve months had just built up and I decided
to take it out on people by descending into a grump.

I had gone walking with what passes for our dog. Mistake. A nice enough animal,
but she's not quite sure what she is – part rat, part rabbit, part psychotic private secretary
to my wife. Her name is Klingon and she's never really warmed to me.

Still, we walked around the oval. She would growl and I'd growl back.

I'd walked around this oval lots of times. There was a playground at one end, where
Stella would play sometimes after school. I listened to her one sunny evening when
she looped the loop around the monkey bars, singing a form of 'Everybody Loves
Somebody'.

There she hung, upside down, and in between giggles she continued the tradition of
the McInnes' deep fondness for Dean Martin songs.

I remembered walking around this oval one afternoon with Sarah and Doug. Sarah
was pregnant with Clem and Doug was just being Doug.

We played a game of Dougie relay, where we would stand about one hundred metres
from each other and call Doug and he would quite happily hare between us both. And
Sarah had laughed; warm and with all her body behind it.

Klingon pulled a little and I tripped over the leash. I yelled at her and she growled back. I pulled on the leash. Then, out of the darkness, a huge humming roar. Above the oval an air ambulance helicopter, like a giant locust, hovering in the night, its bright light shining a wide arc that sharpened into a shrinking ball of white as it descended. Paramedics waited to race the patient to the local hospital; the oval was a landing spot for such emergencies and the event always brought little clumps of neighbourhood spectators.

What looked like a Sleeping Beauty canopy was lifted off the helicopter and wheeled to a spot not far from the ambulance.

I took a catch at mid-on some years ago in that very spot for the local cricket team. Clem, at the age of twelve, was dragged on to make up the numbers. He was a bit nervous and worried about what all the grown-ups would make of him. He was a little shy, too, and didn't want to go out and field so I told him we were all just fat old men.

'You're all grown-ups,' he said.

How long ago did that seem? Occasionally, I'll bump into blokes from the team and they'll invariably talk about that catch. I remembered Clem shaking my hand.

'Good catch! Good catch, Dad!' he said to me. He shook my hand. What an old-fashioned thing to have done. That catch seems ages ago now.

Suddenly, a little kid from the onlookers pointed. 'There's a man in there! In the bubble!'

Inside the canopy was a person, a man. We all stood and looked. Paramedics went about their business. I thought maybe the man in the bubble could see us, standing and staring. What might he have thought? His life had changed that day. Ours? Well, he was something to stare and point at.

What would happen to him? Maybe he was a bit like me. Maybe he'd been in a grump today. I wondered if he'd had enough time to say to his family that he loved them, to speak to the people who mattered. Maybe to let them know he was sorry if he had anything to be sorry for or just that he cared. That people had mattered.

Too often we think life goes on. And we go on with it. People always bang on about the hassles of this time of year — of dealing with families, friends, just people, generally, the silliness of New Year as a new beginning when it's just another day.

I felt my son's hand in mine. Like the day he shook it. I heard my daughter singing as she looped the loop on the monkey bars and I heard my wife's warm laughter.

I looked at the departing ambulance, felt the fragility and randomness of life. I really don't know about New Year's resolutions, but I decided to go home and tell my family how much they meant to me. And I patted Klingon. She growled. And that was okay.